When It's Time to Downsize

The desire to downsize is nothing new. Consider all of the fantasy and science fiction films based on people being miniaturized down to the size of a child's toy—or even a human blood cell. The first thing these tiny people comment on is how big and beautiful everything around them is!

Downsizing our possessions, and our lifestyle, opens our eyes in much the same way. Instead of us getting smaller, it's our responsibilities that shrink. With more time, more financial freedom, and less stress in our lives, we're free to enjoy what matters most...BIG things, like exploring more of the world, continuing to learn and grow, being able to sit and enjoy a sunset, read a book, or spend more time with the people we love.

Whether you want to downsize to a smaller home, shrink your ecological footprint, or simply declutter your closet, *When It's Time to Downsize* will help you reach your goal, one step at a time.

- Pick and choose which topics and projects best fit your needs.
- Work at your own pace.
- Find the inspiration to break long-held habits.
- Learn the secret to being content with less.

Packed with hints, tips, trivia, and hacks, this little book can help you get out from under the stuff that's holding you back from getting the most out of life.

TABLE OF CONTENTS

WANT A BIGGER LIFE?

Think Small!

Thinking small is in! It's a growing trend among millennials, as well as those who find themselves a little further down the road of life. Choosing to downsize not only provides more wiggle room in your budget and your schedule, but in your closet and garage, as well. But downsizing isn't a one-size-fits-all adventure. Each of us has a unique set of reasons behind the desire to pare down.

Which of these reasons hit home for you?

- **Greater financial freedom**
- **Less responsibility**
- **Accommodating changing health concerns**
- **More time with the grandkids**
- **Change in employment or marital status**
- **Less stress and greater peace of mind**
- **Moving an aging parent to a senior living facility**
- **More time for what matters most**
- **Adjusting to the death of a spouse or parent**
- **Reducing your environmental footprint**
- **Less time cleaning the house and mowing the lawn**
- **More freedom to travel**
- **Preparing for retirement**
- **Saying good-bye to clutter**
- **Fulfilling a long-held dream**

What's behind *your* desire to downsize? Understanding your Why will help you determine the most efficient How. In the space below, write out your own personal Think Small Vision Statement. Summarize what you hope to gain by letting go of what you're holding onto right now.

_____

_____

_____

_____

_____

_____

_____

_____

_____

_____

_____

Go ahead. Dare to think small. You'll be amazed at the ways your world will expand!

Where to Begin?

Thinking small can become a big job. It can be so overwhelming, that some people quit before they even begin. But you're not one of them! That's because you have a plan. Well, you WILL have a plan once you work your way through this helpful book. As you do, keep your Vision Statement in mind. You're working toward something that will make your life more manageable and enjoyable. That's a worthy goal!

So, where should you begin? By breaking your big job down into bite-sized jobs. One systematic way of doing that is to print off monthly calendar sheets on your computer. (Or purchase a calendar with extra-large grids.) If you have a set end date for downsizing (such as when you want to put your home on the market), divide the time between that date and today into weeks. Make a list of the jobs you need to complete. Then, divide those jobs, estimating how long each job will take you to complete, by your available weeks.

If your downsizing goals have no set time limit, set one. Block out a designated number of hours, or number of tasks, to complete each week. Write them on your calendar. This will help keep you on task, so downsizing doesn't wind up stealing your free time, instead of freeing you up to do more of what you love.

Post your "TO DOwnsize" calendar somewhere you can readily see it. Each time you complete one of your bite-sized jobs, cross it off with great gusto! Go YOU!!!!

To help get you started, here is a sample list of bite-sized jobs you may want to include on your "TO DOwnsize" calendar. Personalize your list to suit your own needs and Vision Statement. First, list every room or area of your house that you want to declutter/downsize. Then, break down each room into a list of bite-sized jobs.

BEDROOM
Closet
Dresser
Nightstands
Jewelry box
Under bed

KITCHEN
Pantry
Freezer
Refrigerator
Dishes
Pots and pans
Cooking utensils
Silverware drawer
Cookbooks
Linens
Seasonal tableware or decor
Under the sink

LIVING ROOM
Knickknacks
Old magazines
Any cabinet with doors or drawers

OFFICE or HOBBY ROOM
Desk
Old tax returns and papers
Bookcase
Office supplies

GARAGE or SHED
Tools
Anything stored in bins
Seasonal decorations

BATHROOM
Cosmetics
Toiletries
Linens

BASEMENT
ATTIC
HALL CLOSET
LAUNDRY ROOM
BEDROOM(S), GUEST ROOM(S), KIDS ROOM(S)
FRONT YARD
BACKYARD
TOYS
(for kids or grandkids)

MISC.
Collectibles
Photos and albums
Letters
Artwork
Wrapping paper & greeting cards
Junk drawers
Memorabilia

✓ Check This Out

Do not begin downsizing by tackling emotionally sentimental items, such as photos, old letters, baby clothes you've held onto for thirty years, or your cherished collection of vintage garden gnomes. Choose something more neutral, like the pantry or bedroom closet, to get started. Save sorting sentimental items for when you're feeling well-rested, positively motivated, and energized.

Right about now, you may be chomping at the bit to get to work. Enough with all of this planning and paperwork! The sooner you get started, the sooner you'll be finished, right? Yes and no. Chances are, if you start right in, opening the cupboard nearest your dominant hand and throwing things willy-nilly, you'll find you've made a bigger mess than the one you find yourself in right now. Your initial exuberance may lead you to get rid of things that a week later you'll wish you had, or lead you to take everything out—and then put it back in a more organized manner, without really purging anything. Neither of these methods will get you where you want to go in terms of your Vision Statement.

So, let's begin with an area you use every day...your bedroom closet.

Behind Closed Doors

Cue the laugh track. Someone innocently opens a closet door and is promptly buried beneath an avalanche of coats, skis, cleaning supplies, stuffed animals, rolls of gift wrap...you name it. This scene may have played well to sitcom audiences in days gone by, but it isn't all that funny when that closet just so happens to be yours.

Just because we can still close a closet door doesn't mean that everything behind it is useful or necessary. It's also one reason why a closet is a great place to start downsizing. It's not even a whole room. It's one, small, enclosed area, hidden from public view. It's something you can get under control in a relatively short amount of time—depending on the size of your closet and your personal inclination toward hoarding.

In addition, since your closet is one door you open every morning, conquering this source of clutter can be a daily visual reminder of how thinking small can yield big results.

Here are a few tips to get started:

- Turn on some music to help keep you feeling upbeat.

- Take EVERYTHING out of the closet. (Yes, everything!) Put it on the floor or your bed. This will help you see more clearly how much you really own.

- Remind yourself that each item has only three options: Closet, Give It Away, or Discard.

- Anything you absolutely love, and wear on a regular basis, return to your Closet.

- Anything you like, but don't wear very often, try on. Check yourself out in a full-length mirror. Do you like how it looks on you? Do you like how you feel when you're wearing it? If there's any hesitation on your part, put it in the Give Away pile. If it's a bona-fide winner, return it to your Closet.

- Anything that doesn't fit (unless you happen to be pregnant!) goes in the Give Away pile.

- Anything you're holding onto for sentimental reasons (such as, those amazing stilettos that look so cool but are impossible to wear, that dress that made you look so skinny—when you wore it 10 years ago, the worn out t-shirt you bought at your first live concert, that "dry clean only" sweater you love but never wear, and even your wedding dress—if you do not have daughters who may want to wear it someday). If you do not wear it regularly, it is clutter—not clothing. If it's too badly worn, Discard it. If someone else could use it, Give It Away.

If you love to shop, or you're someone who hesitates to part with anything that doesn't sport a hole larger than the size of your fist, your wardrobe can easily expand far beyond what you actually wear. If this describes you, try to reduce what's in your closet by at least 50%. If you have ten pair of black pants, whittle that number down to your five favorites, etc. THEN, resolve to not add anything new to your Closet, unless you Give Away or Discard another item to free up a hanger.

Hang It Up

Once you do the hard work of weeding through your closet, it's time to consider how you care for what you keep. The better care you take of what you own, the longer you'll be able to use it, the less time you'll spend shopping to replace it, and the more discretionary money you'll have on hand when you need it—like to buy better hangers!

Wire hangers are inexpensive and seem to breed like rabbits in dark closets. However, they often leave lumps, bumps and creases on clothing. They can also snag delicate materials, they tangle as easily as Christmas lights, and they can rust in damp or humid climates, leaving stains on your clothing that you cannot remove. Yes, they are thin—which allows you to squeeze more into your closet. But we're talking about cutting down on clutter, not squeezing more stuff into less space.

Trading out the wire hangers in your closet for plastic ones will give your clothing more room to hang wrinkle-free. You can even find hangers that are biodegradable and compostable! One easy way to make the switch is to purchase one package of non-wire hangers each time you're at a big-box store. In dollar stores, you can sometimes purchase about 20 hangers for $2. That's less than a fancy coffee! So, just say NO to wire hangers. It's one small way to help you keep your closet under control, while being kinder to your clothing at the same time.

Although most charities do not accept wire hangers, most dry cleaners do. You can also drop them off as scrap metal at the dump for recycling.

HINT: Is there clothing in your closet that it still sporting its original tag? This is a shopping addiction warning sign! Don't purchase something simply because it's on sale or you're having a bad day and that cute little vest makes you smile. Shop for what you'll actually wear. Your closet, and your budget, will thank you for it.

Unless you wear clothing for work, such as suits that need to be dry cleaned, avoid purchasing anything in the future with a care label that says, "Dry Clean Only." Not only does the cost of dry cleaning raise the price of any item you buy, you may often neglect wearing these items, because you don't want to spend the extra time and money it takes to care for them. Not to mention that most dry cleaners use toxic chemicals on your clothing which can cause a health risk over time.

Here are a couple of tips to help you keep your closet under control:

- To continue weeding out your closet with little effort, turn all of the hangers around (with the open end of the hook facing away from the wall) in your closet. When you wear an item of clothing, turn the hanger back around the right direction. At the end of the season, see which hangers have NOT been turned around. Carefully consider whether those items should be discarded or given away.

- If you are a fashionista who enjoys wearing trendy items, buy inexpensive ones, since you'll only wear them for a season or two before they will be out of style.

- Scrutinize your shoes, outerwear, and accessories as carefully as you have your clothing. Does it fit your body, your lifestyle, and your available space? If not, add to your Give Away or Discard pile.

- When purchasing specialty items, such as holiday sweaters, fancy dresses (unless you live a fancy, party kind of life!), or designer high heels, calculate their REAL cost before adding them to your closet. Suppose the light-up Santa sweater cost $60 and you will wear it about four times during the holiday season for about three years. That means it will cost you $5 every time you wear it—not including dry cleaning costs. Compare that with a pair of $60 jeans that you'll wear twice a week for two years—or more. The jeans will cost less than 30 cents each time you wear them. Or consider what that means for the $200+ designer heels or Dry Clean Only beaded dress you want to wear for New Year's Eve? How you spend your money is up to you. Just remember to pay attention to the Big Picture, when you're trying to Think Small.

Ways to Say Good-Bye

so long *fare well* *bye-bye*

Most people think of donating their clothing to charity when they clean out their closet. But that's not the only option. First, consider that many charities receive more clothing than they can sell. Some of it even ends up in landfills.

Here are a few other Give Away options:

- **Share the wealth with your friends.** Invite them to clean out their own closets and bring their gently used clothing to a Give 'n Take party. (You may want to set a limit of 20 pieces of clothing per person.) Provide snacks, a shopping bag, and a fun, fashion-friendly atmosphere. Set up a bedroom or basement where your guests can try on each other's clothing and take home their favorites. (You may want to borrow some full-length mirrors to set around the room.) Encourage your guests to only take what they will use. Gather what's left over and donate it to charity. Why not do the same with kitchenware, art work, books, etc.? It's a fun way to shop without spending a dime.

- **Host a garage sale and give** all of the proceeds to charity.

- **Have a Downsizing Party.** Put all of the things you love, but don't use, or won't fit into a smaller home, on display. Then invite your friends over and let them take what they like. This way, you know the things you care about are going to a good home where they will be enjoyed.

- **Keep Give Away bags in your car for the homeless.** Each could contain a tee shirt, jacket or coat, pair of socks, bottle of water, and any mini-toiletries you've collected from out-of-town lodging.

- **Connect with local charities that provide clothing free of charge to women who need a fresh start.**

- **Donate any clothing that is no longer wearable to charities that recycle it into rags.**

Check This Out

If you're downsizing to a smaller home, consider the size of the closet when choosing your future bedroom. It's tempting to want a larger, walk-in closet, even in a smaller home. Just remember that having a large closet is like keeping a pair of "fat pants" in your wardrobe. It's an open invitation to grow to fit into it!

When You Can't Let Go...

There are some items of clothing, like a wedding dress, tee-shirt commemorating a favorite trip or personal achievement, even that favorite pair of flannel pjs that you've loved to death, that are really tough to part with. Why not repurpose them into something useful, instead of allowing them to simply take up room in your closet? The internet abounds with DIY projects that transform used clothing into something fun and useful. That way you can hold onto your memories, or pass them onto your children or grandkids, in a fresh, new way.

Here are just a few ideas to get you started:

- Instead of hanging onto your wedding dress, commemorative tee-shirts, or that fancy, out-of-style cocktail dress with the shoulder pads, turn them into stuffed animals for the grandkids. Include a gift card that explains to the child the significance of their new "stuffie."

- Use the front of old concert or travel tee-shirts to make a quilt.

- Transform an old tee-shirt into a reusable grocery bag with just a few straight seams.

- Make elegant scarves or sachets (filled with dried lavender) from former formalwear.

- Turn an old pair of jeans into a door draft stopper. Turn one leg of the jeans inside-out. Insert a foam pool float cylinder and pin the jeans to fit snugly. Remove pool float. Sew a seam along pin guidelines. Trim jeans to fit width of a drafty doorframe. Trim the float one inch shorter. Turn the jeans right-side out and insert the pool float. Seam the ends.

- Pass on some of your former favorite apparel (including hats, costume jewelry, and shoes) to the grandkids, or a day care center, to use to play dress up.

- Turn your favorite sweater or old flannel pjs into a cozy pillow.

HINT: The word nostalgia comes from two Greek words: nostos, which means "return home" and algos, which means "pain." If the closet you happen to be cleaning out is that of a recently deceased parent, recognize that closet will hold a lot more than clothing. It will hold decades of memories. If you have siblings (or other family members) you feel close to and comfortable with, tackling this task together can be a positive, healing activity, a time to grieve and reminisce. Just realize that cleaning out a closet, a room in an assisted living facility, or the entire family home, will be taxing physically, mentally, and emotionally. Schedule in chunks of "me" time to help keep your energy up. Stop for a cup of tea. Go see a movie. Take a nap or a bubble bath. Taking care of yourself is a vital part of taking care of others.

Finishing Touches

Downsizing and organizing your bedroom is a major coup to Thinking Small. After all, this is where your brain and your body rest up to face a new day. The more it feels like a peaceful place to retreat, instead of a garage sale waiting to happen, the less stress you will feel when you enter it. This means a better chance for a good night's sleep!

Once you've tackled the most difficult part—the closet—go ahead and finish off the other nooks and crannies. Even cleaning out one drawer a day will help you make great strides, in relatively little time, toward your decluttering goals. Remember to clean underneath the bed. It's a great place to store seasonal clothing IF you actually use it when the season arrives. But if the dust bunnies under your bed have overrun what's hiding beneath it, perhaps it's time to make a literal clean sweep and keep that spot open and empty.

One spot that deserves a little extra time and thought is your nightstand. What do you keep beside your bed—and why? The nightstand is a great place for a reading light, a novel or crossword book, reading glasses (if you need them), and perhaps a photo of those closest to your heart. Other than that, keep it clutter-free. It's best to keep your alarm clock on a dresser across the room, so you have to actually get yourself out of bed, instead of continuing to hit the snooze button, when it goes off in the morning.

The same holds true for your cell phone. Recharge it across the room on your dresser, instead of keeping it close at hand. If you're having trouble falling asleep, it's too tempting to check texts, social media, or do a bit of online shopping when it's within reach. Also, the blue light from your cell phone disrupts your melatonin, which in turn disrupts your sleep cycle.

Having a television in your bedroom can have much the same effect. Not only does it make you more prone to falling asleep while the TV is on, which negatively effects the quality of your sleep, but it raises your electricity and cable provider costs. Using separate rooms of your home for separate activities is one way to keep clutter from flowing freely from one room to the next. Sleep in your bedroom. Enjoy your screen time somewhere else.

Let's Mention the Unmentionables...

Speaking of sleep, when's the last time you saw the bottom of your pajama and lingerie drawer? Or, for that matter, sorted through your intimate apparel? Elastic has a shelf life—and so should anything that depends on that stretch to hold it in place. This includes pjs, bras, socks, tights, hose, camisoles, and "under-things". Out of sight is not out of mind if you're constantly tugging and pulling to reposition undergarments that have long passed their expiration date.

Retain enough underwear to keep you clothed in between laundry days, with a few extras to spare. Toss the stretched out, ill-fitting, tattered remnants of what remains. As for pajamas and nightgowns, two to three for each season should suffice. As for those holiday pajamas, remember Christmas only comes once a year—so plan accordingly.

Do yourself and your clothing a favor, whether it's underwear or outerwear. Treat it kindly. It's an investment—not only a financial one, but an investment of your time. The better care you take of it, the longer you will be able to use it, and the better you will look wearing it.

- **Don't hang sweaters. They will stretch out and you'll have pointy hanger marks on your shoulders when you wear them. Instead, fold sweaters in half, cross the arms in front, and stack them in a drawer or on a shelf in your closet.**

- **Use the delicate cycle on your washing machine for almost everything other than jeans, sheets, and towels.**

- **Use a hamper, not the bedroom floor, to keep your dirty clothes until laundry day.**

- **Hang up what needs to be hung in a closet where there's enough room for clothing to hang freely. If your closet is packed so tightly that items can "hang" without a hanger, it's time to downsize your wardrobe!**

- **Use a drying rack to air dry lingerie, sweaters, and delicate clothing. They will wear longer, and look better, if they aren't repeatedly heated and beaten to death in the dryer.**

- Practice what we teach kids to do each day: put your clothes away and make your bed. It will help keep your bedroom a place you look forward to falling asleep in each night!

- Do the laundry when you're available to take items directly out of the dryer and hang them or fold them. That will prevent having to iron items unnecessarily or looking like a rumpled mess when you get dressed in the morning.

The Land of Lost Socks

No one really knows where all of those single socks go, the ones that mysteriously vanish somewhere between the washer, dryer, and your underwear drawer. Some speculate they elope with plastic food storage containers, leaving a trail of mismatched socks and lids in their wake. So, what do you do with a clean single sock? Here are a just a few ideas!

- Use socks that no longer have a mate as dust cloths. Put your hand inside and swipe up dust in a jiffy!

- Fill a knee sock about half full with clean, unscented kitty litter. Tie the free end of the sock in a knot. Place the sock on the dashboard of your car (and one under the back window, if you desire) when you park. Voila! This sock dehumidifier will absorb excess moisture in your car, preventing your windows from fogging up.

- Help the grandkids make puppets with single socks and random buttons.

- Cut a thumb opening in the heel of a warm, winter sock. Put it on your hand and mark where your knuckles are. Cut off the end. Use your mismatched arm warmers when you read.

- If your downsizing includes a move, place small, breakable items inside socks to keep them protected during transit.

- Place your shoes inside them in your luggage when you travel.

- Use them to store loose pieces in board games.

- If you're painting, put a pair of socks over your shoes to keep them splatter-free.

- To make an instant cat toy, fill a sock with catnip and tie the open end.

- Measure your favorite coffee or tea mug. Cut the top section off of the sock to fit. Poof! A mug cozy to help keep your favorite hot drink warmer longer!

The Paper Chase

After getting your bedroom under control, it's time to tackle random paper clutter. Left unchecked, it can multiply like proverbial rabbits into stacks, piles, and bulging files. Unfortunately, simply clearing off every flat surface in your home isn't the answer. Only new habits can ultimately conquer those paper rabbits!

But first things first. Bring all of your piled papers into one room. Don't forget those hiding in junk drawers or fastened to your fridge with decorative magnets. Separate them into what needs to be recycled, shredded, scanned, or filed. If you need some help deciding what goes into which pile, here are a few guidelines as to what you do NOT need to hold onto any longer:

- **OWNERS' MANUALS. Most manuals** for appliances, electronics, camera's, etc. are available online. So why clutter up your home with a paper copy? Download a PDF of the manual from the product's website on the internet and store the digital copy in a "Owner's Manual" file on your computer. Then, recycle the physical copy.

- **OLD ADDRESS LABELS. If you don't** live there, you don't need these. Shred them, along with other paper work that carries personal info from a previous address.

- **EXPIRED COUPONS. This may seem** like a no brainer, but expired coupons are simply taking up space. Military families are allowed to use coupons up to 6 months beyond their expiration date. If this does not describe you, you can donate recently expired coupons to the nearest military facility.

- **KIDS ARTWORK. During their early** school years, kids and grandkids create countless works of art. But unless you have enough room in your home to classify as a bona fide museum, it's best to save only one or two pieces each year from each child. If you want to save them in a bin during the school year, choose which masterpieces make the cut at the beginning of summer vacation. Dispose of the rest—when and where your kids can't find them! Better yet, scan the artwork and save the image on your computer. Not only does this save you from paper clutter but also allows you to print them at a later date. This way you can put them in an album or a frame, or even turn them into jigsaw puzzles, a deck of playing cards, refrigerator magnets, or Christmas ornaments through a variety of online sites.

- **MAGAZINES.** It's so tempting to save those old issues of National Geographic or Smithsonian magazine. "Someday, they'll be worth something!" you tell yourself. While it's true that any issue of National Geographic published before 1905 is worth about $200, most of the magazines we're holding onto are not worth the price of the paper they're printed on. Sure, they may be fun to look at now and again. But when was the last time you did? Sometimes, it's tough to even have time to read the latest issue. Why not pass on or recycle that stack you have on hand? Donate back issues to a school, library, hospital, or retirement home. (Tear off the section that displays your address before donating.) And if you're receiving a magazine in the mail and several months go by and you've never picked it up to read, stop your subscription. Even if it's at a great rate! Consider an online subscription, instead. No clutter, no trees cut down to print it, and no guilt if you don't get around to reading it.

- **NEWSPAPERS.** Toss this into recycling every day as soon as you've read it. Don't save unread papers for tomorrow. It's old news. If you want to save a crossword puzzle, tear out that page. Put crosswords in a file folder and save them to take on vacation or complete in your spare time. Or consider subscribing to a digital version of the paper. Save a tree and your home from additional paper clutter.

- **RECEIPTS.** Unless you need to save them for a warranty or tax purposes, shred them.

- **MAIL.** When you pick up the mail each day, sort it next to a paper shredder and recycle basket. Put bills you need to pay or cards you need to answer in an ACTION file or box. If you receive an invitation, R.S.V.P. to it A.S.A.P! Add the details to your calendar, so you can recycle the invitation right away. Do the same with flyers announcing upcoming events you'd like to attend. With junk mail, if an envelope has a cellophane window or any decoration, such as glitter or foil, remove it before recycling it. Shred anything that contains personal info. Also, take a few minutes to reduce the amount of junk mail you receive each day by unsubscribing to catalogs, charities, non-profits, and other organizations you no longer wish to hear from.

- **CATALOGS.** These can stack up in no time, particularly around the Christmas season. If you see something you may like to order in the future, tear out the page (which usually has the website of the vendor printed at the bottom. If not, write it on the page). Then place it in a "To Purchase" file. Recycle the rest of the catalog.

- **OLD GREETING CARDS AND LETTERS.** In this digital age of emails, e-cards, and texts, it's tempting to save actual handwritten notes, greeting cards, and letters. But just because something is valuable emotionally, doesn't make it valuable enough to save indefinitely. If you have the room to store this kind of memorabilia in the garage, attic, basement, or on a top shelf of a closet, try and keep it contained to a single box or plastic bin.

- **OLD PAID BILLS.** If they're more than three months old, and you don't need them for tax purposes, shred them. As for NEW bills, bank statements, and reciepts needed for taxes; why not sign up to go paperless from here on out? Set up automatic payments on your recurring bills and you'll never have to think about them, or handle that extra piece of paper, again!

File It, Don't Pile It!

There are some paper documents that are important to KEEP. Just be sure to file them, not pile them. These include: medical records, recent tax-related documents and receipts, insurance policies, loan documents, and warranties with necessary receipts attached. Once again, you may have access to some of these online. If you do, shred the paper copies. You can also scan them all and save them digitally. Just make certain you have them backed up in the cloud or on a separate hard drive in case your computer crashes.

A Time to File, and a Time to Shred

Shredding documents that are no longer necessary, but contain personal information, is a wise move. But whether or not you can put shredded paper into your recycling bin depends upon your curbside recycler. Most will not accept it. Those that do, may ask you to put it into plastic bags beforehand— or send it straight to the landfill if it's in a plastic bag. Search online to find the preferred method of recycling shredded paper in your area.

If you do not own a paper shredder, go online to find the location most convenient for you to drop off for bulk shredding. Some even have "free shred" days. Others may charge you by the pound.

If you're considering purchasing your own paper shredder, choose one that handles several pages at a time and sits directly on top of a trash can. You may also want to consider one that shreds thicker items, such as credit cards. Always remember to remove staples before putting anything through a personal shredder, unless it's designed to handle them. If you're dropping paper off at a bulk shredding facility, you can leave the staples in place.

Why Recycling Paper Matters

Did you know that the single oldest living thing on earth is a tree? Up until 2013, it was believed to be a bristlecone pine named Methuselah growing in California's White Mountains. It's over 4,700 years old. That means it was alive and growing when the Egyptians built the pyramids! That deserves a little respect. However, a bristlecone pine that is over 5,000 years old was discovered in the same area. Its location is being kept secret to help protect this venerable old bristlecone.

Most trees are much more anonymous—and their lifetimes are much briefer—than Methuselah and friends. Each year, four billion trees are cut around the world to be used by the paper industry. That is 35% of all trees harvested. You'd think that our current digital age would reduce the number of trees cut down each year for paper products. However, the world's consumption of trees has increased 400% over the last 40 years. That is 2.47 billion trees cut down each day.

Each ton of recycled paper saves 17 trees. It also saves 380 gallons of oil, three cubic yards of landfill space, 4000 kilowatts of energy, and 7000 gallons of water that would have been used to produce new, unrecycled paper—as well as 60 pounds of additional air pollution! Those same 17 trees would also absorb about 250 pounds of carbon dioxide from the air in our atmosphere every single year. Those are hard-working trees!

Did you know that if we simply recycled all of the newspapers printed in the U.S. each year, we'd save 250,000,000 trees? We may not save quite that many by simply recycling the paper clutter we've accumulated around our home, but every little bit helps. So, let's make recycling a helpful habit we acquire as we strive to Think Small!

Safely Disposing of Odds and Ends

As we're downsizing, there are a lot of other things we'll come across that we no longer need or want, and we'll be tempted to simply toss them into the trash. However, many things in our homes can adversely affect the environment if we do not dispose of them properly.

Take paint, for example. Oil-based paint is considered a hazardous waste product and is toxic to people, as well as the environment. It needs to be taken to an HHW (Household Hazardous Waste) facility to be disposed of safely. However, latex paint can be disposed of in your own trash can. Let it harden and dry first. If you have a large amount, adding cat litter or sand will help it harden more quickly. Better yet, take dried cans of latex paint (without any cat litter added!) to a local recycling facility where it can be repurposed into new paint!

Batteries and fluorescent light bulbs need to join oil-based paints in being taken to a HHW disposal facility. Computers and old cell phones also need special care. Once you've wiped their information clean, many electronics stores will dispose of them safely. Or, a variety of charities will accept them to refurbish and then donate to people who can use them.

Check This Out

Did you know that recycling one aluminum can could save enough energy to run your television for three hours? In addition, steel and tin cans can be recycled into rebar, bicycle parts and appliances. Junk mail can be recycled into roofing shingles and paper towel rolls. Recycled notebook and computer paper can be made into facial tissue, toilet paper, and new notebook paper.

Recycling 101

Ultimately, it would be great to aim for a zero-waste home, one where composting, recycling, repurposing, and reusing, are an eco-friendly way of life. However, most of us aren't there yet. We feel pretty good about the fact that we get around to separating our trash from our recyclables. But, are we doing it correctly?

Recycling reduces landfills, saves energy, preserves natural resources, protects wildlife, and reduces greenhouse gas emissions. However, if even one house recycles incorrectly, it could contaminate an entire truck load of neighborhood recycling. Once contaminated, recyclables wind up back in the landfill.

One of the main reasons people say they don't recycle is that they don't have enough space. Let's not downsize our life so much that we don't save room for recycling. We owe it to our planet and future generations to take a few minutes, and a little bit of space, to recycle what we can.

Here are a few tips for making sure what you recycle doesn't end up in the landfill.

DO RECYCLE:

- **PAPER:** newspaper, magazines and catalogs, junk mail, cardboard, frozen food packaging (clean), wrapping paper, and paper bags.

- **CANS:** aluminum, tin, steel, and aerosol (empty, without pressure). Check with your local recycler to see if clean tin foil is accepted—and consider buying recycled aluminum foil in the future.

- **UNBROKEN GLASS:** Bottles and jars. (Do NOT put broken light bulbs or window glass in recycling.)

- **PLASTIC:** milk (clean), shampoo (clean), and water bottles, stamped with #1 through 7. Plastic soda bottles can also be recycled, but recycling plants vary as to whether their caps can or not. Check with your local recycler for guidelines.

- **RECYCLABLE TAKE-OUT FOOD CONTAINERS:** thoroughly rinsed. Any grease or food waste will contaminate them.

DO NOT PUT IN RECYCLING:

- **DISPOSABLE COFFEE CUPS AND JUICE BOXES:** These are lined with plastic. Some coffee cup lids and juice boxes may be recyclable. Check with your local recycler for guidelines.

- **STYROFOAM:** Try to avoid using it whenever possible, since it isn't biodegradable and takes 500 years to break down in a landfill. However, if you receive some as packing material, reuse it.

- **GARDEN WASTE:** Nope. Just don't. That includes wood of any kind.

- **PLASTIC BAGS:** While your local recycler usually cannot accommodate flexible plastic bags, such as grocery, produce, or bread bags, grocery stores often accept them to recycle.

- **GREASE STAINED PIZZA BOXES:** If the lid is grease and food-free, tear it off and throw that into recycling.

- **USED DIAPERS, NAPKINS AND PAPER TOWELS, NEEDLES AND MEDICAL WASTE:** Yup, some people do it. Don't be one of them.

Time to Dream...

After all of your diligent downsizing, perhaps now's an opportune moment to take a time-out…and dream a little! Close your eyes and ask yourself, "What does my 'dream home' look like?" What first pops into your mind? A chateau in the south of France? A secluded lakeside cabin? A little grass hut nestled into the sand of your favorite beach? Don't think about the finances or feasibility of that home right now. Just let your desires and imagination wander.

When it comes to finding a home, the familiar chant of real estate agents everywhere is "location, location, location!" You can change out the counter-tops, paint a wall, or update fixtures. Often, you can even add more square footage. But unless your dream abode is a mobile home, it's going to stay right where it's built.

So, if your downsizing includes changing your address, first consider "where" before you settle on "what." Do you want to stay in the same, familiar area you live in now? Do you want to move closer to grandchildren? Are you ready to pull up stakes and move from the mountains to the seashore, from cold weather to warmer climes?

If you're longing for a chateau in France, but your lottery ticket hasn't paid off yet, consider what it is about southern France that draws you? Verdant landscapes? A slower pace of life? A bit of adventure? Living in a home that exudes rustic charm and holds a bit of history within its walls?

Once you've figured out what it is about your dream location that appeals to you, if that location is not practical for your budget or lifestyle, you can often find a place that has some similar characteristics that may be a more realistic fit. To help you think through this process, pour yourself a cup of coffee or tea (and add a scone, to help you dream BIG while still trying to think SMALL) and fill out the Dream Home Worksheet.

Dream Home
LOCATION, LOCATION, LOCATION

What setting do I picture when I think of my dream home?

_____

_____

_____

_____

_____

_____

What specific characteristics appeal to me about that location?

_____

_____

_____

_____

_____

_____

If my dream home's location isn't realistic for my budget and/or my lifestyle, what other areas share some of the characteristics I'm drawn to most?

_____

_____

_____

_____

_____

_____

_____

_____

_____

My Location Wish List
(For instance: mature trees, accessibility to grocery store, walkable neighborhood, retirement community, etc.)

_____

_____

_____

_____

_____

_____

_____

_____

_____

Now, go back over your wish list and put a star next to any specific features you feel are a "must have," as opposed to simply a "it would be nice."

Check This Out

Now that you've spent some time picturing WHERE your dream home would be, it's time to consider WHAT that home will be like. If downsizing is one of your goals, square footage should be a major consideration. If you're considering the drastic downsize of moving to a "tiny home," it's best to spend at least several weeks living in a vacation rental that's about the same size as the miniature home of your dreams. For many people, cozy can become claustrophobic in just a matter of weeks.

According to the current trend, a true "tiny" house is generally categorized as anything less than 500 sq. feet, with "micro" homes as small as 80 sq. feet. A "small" house is anything between 500 and 1,000 feet. Many one to two-bedroom apartments and condominiums are under 1,000 square feet, so the difference between "small" and "tiny" is actually a big one.

Dream Home
SIZE MATTERS

Square footage of my current home:

_____

Realistic goal square footage for my downsized dream home:

_____

Properties I'd consider:

____ single family home

____ condo or townhome

____ apartment

____ mobile home

____ tiny home (or small home)

Below each room, add any specific amenities you'd love your downsized dream home to include, such as a walk-in closet, fireplace, or soaking tub.

Rooms you want in your downsized dream home:

____ bedrooms

_____

____ bathrooms (full or half?)

_____

____ kitchen

_____

____ dining room

_____

____ formal living room

_____

____ family room

_____

____ laundry room

_____

____ basement

_____

____ garage

_____

____ additional rooms
(such as an office, open loft area, etc.)

_____

The Great Outdoors

A home is more than what lies inside its walls. It's also the outdoor space that surrounds it. One downsizing dream people often hold is saying good-bye to raking leaves and mowing the lawn. Others look forward to spending more time puttering around a garden. Which camp do YOU fall into?

If you like the beauty of a yard, but don't want the hassle of caring for it, downsizing to a townhome or condo may be the perfect choice for you. Monthly HOA (Home Owners Association) fees often include landscape maintenance, trash service, snow removal, and insurance and maintenance for the exterior of your property. Some HOAs also include access to a pool, gym, barbeque grills, and a clubhouse that can be rented out for special occasions. All you need to add is a "walls in" insurance policy to cover the inside of your property.

While HOAs can help downsize your personal responsibility, their fees can increase every year. Also, if there's major damage to the complex from natural disasters like a hail storm or flood, they may charge a Special Assessment fee which could cost you thousands of dollars. It's wise to ask for a special rider on your "walls in" insurance policy that covers this scenario, so all you'll have to come up with is your deductible.

In contrast, if you're the type who loves to get down and dirty in the garden, that doesn't mean you're locked in to only moving to a property with a yard. Communal gardens are becoming more prevalent not only in urban areas, but even in the suburbs. City parks sometimes offer small plots of land you can rent and then plant to your heart's content. And don't discount the satisfaction of a window garden or potted plants on a patio or balcony! There's plenty of opportunities to "grow" even if you're trying to shrink your square footage.

Dream Home
ON THE OUTSIDE

When dreaming of the perfect downsized home, which styles come to mind most often?

____ Ranch   ____ Craftsman

____ Split Level   ____ Southwestern Pueblo

____ Modern/Contemporary   ____ Cottage/Bungalow

____ Victorian   ____ Other

The type of lot that appeals to me most:
(List specifics, such as a corner lot, end unit or first floor for a condo, backs up to open space, not on a busy street, etc.)

_____

My Front Yard Wish List:

_____
_____
_____
_____

My Backyard Wish List:

_____
_____
_____
_____

Any other outdoor features I'd love to have:

_____
_____
_____
_____

Let's Talk Storage

Since downsizing is your primary goal, keep that goal in mind as you dream of a new home. Squishing the same amount of stuff into smaller square footage isn't downsizing, or even organizing. It's deceiving yourself. While it's wonderful to have a home with ample storage space, filling your garage, basement, or backyard shed to the brim is still hoarding—even if you aren't featured on a reality television show. Just because something's hidden from view, doesn't render it nonexistent.

So, take a few moments and go back over the Dream Home Worksheets you've completed. Star or highlight everything you NEED, as opposed to what you WANT. This doesn't mean your dreams don't matter, or that you shouldn't try to fulfill them. It's simply a reminder to keep those dreams in perspective.

We've spent some time dreaming about making a big move to a smaller space, but let's get back to work right where we live. Once your bedroom and paper clutter is under control, it's time to turn your attention to your storage areas—regardless of how daunting that thought may be!

First up? If you're paying money each month to rent a storage unit, it's time to clean it out. Permanently. Other than renting offsite storage for temporary use (such as when you're in between moves or remodeling your home), a storage unit is basically a form of procrastination. Instead of dealing with it, you're concealing it! Not only that, you're wasting money that could be spent in better ways, such as paying off any outstanding debt or building up your savings to prepare for unforeseen expenses.

But before you get rid of a storage unit, you have to clean it out. The same process you used to clean your closet, works for offsite storage, a tool shed, attic, basement, or garage. First, remove every item from your storage space. If there are items that are too large or heavy to move easily, put a sticky note on them to designate which pile they belong in: Keep, Give Away, Discard or Sell. Make certain if that sticky note does not say "Keep," you find the help you need to get that item to its designated destination by a set date. Your downsizing isn't complete until everything is in its proper place, which for some items is a place that is far, far away from your own storage space!

Be ruthless as you sort through your stored items. If you have 2 shovels, keep the one that's in the best condition and donate or sell the other. If you haven't used something in over a year, you probably won't use it this year either—so get rid of it. If you have "someday" items, such as a lawn mower you haven't used since you xeriscaped, but you hope that someday you'll have a small patch of green to mow, first check to see if it still works. If it's a big ticket item, such as a lawn mower or sewing machine, it still works, you have ample space to store it, and you can see yourself using it sometime in the next year, keep it. But if it's still sitting in the same spot collecting dust next year, you may want to change that item from Keep to Give Away, Discard or Sell.

There's no better time to give your garage a thorough cleaning than when you're sorting through everything that has been filling it.

Here are a couple of quick and easy cleaning tips:

- **Always start from the top and work down. That way dust and dirt falls down onto surfaces that you haven't yet cleaned.**

- **Use a broom to clear away any cobwebs hiding in the corners or ceiling.**

- **Wipe down light fixtures, garage door hardware, and any windows.**

- **If you're really ready to tidy up, wipe down the walls with a large car wash sponge. Dry with an old towel.**

- **Starting from the back of the garage, use a push broom to sweep anything on the floor toward the garage door. Dispose of the dirt and debris.**

- **Give the floor a thorough mopping.**

- **After the floor dries, scrub away any oil stains on the floor with a wire brush. Use commercial oil stain remover, if needed.**

- **If your garage floor is not painted, this is a great time to do it! This will make the floor easier to sweep or mop, as well as extend the life of the concrete by preventing moisture from seeping into any cracks you may have by sealing them. Remember to start from a back corner and work your way to the opposite corner nearest the door.**

Four Bins for the Win!

Stackable plastic containers are not only useful to keep your garage tidy, they can help out in your home, as well. Try the four-bin method. (If you want your home décor to look a little more "fashion forward," use baskets, instead of plastic tubs.)

1) Keep one bin inside, somewhere convenient, but relatively out of sight. A good spot is near the back door, inside a walk-in pantry, or at the bottom of a staircase. If you get busy during the day, toss items that need to be put away somewhere else in your home in this bin. For instance, papers you've received in the mail that need to be filed or dirty socks that someone left near the couch. First thing in the morning or every evening before you go to bed, put the things in this bin in their proper place.

2) Place one bin in the garage where you keep items that need a bit of maintenance or repair, such as a shirt that's missing a button, a chipped mug that needs to be glued, or shoes that need to be polished. Schedule time once a week to clean out this bin by taking care of these little odd jobs.

3) Keep a bin in the garage where you put items you wish to donate. Whenever this bin gets full, run by your favorite charity to drop off your gently used items.

4) If you do not have recycling picked up at your home along with your trash, keep a bin in the garage where you place all of your recyclables, such as newspapers, empty cans and bottles. When it gets full, take it to a recycling center.

If you're serious about using your storage space well, mount ceiling hooks to hold bicycles, camping gear, and sporting equipment. Install shelving to keep stackable plastic containers off the floor. Place containers that hold items you're storing for the long haul (such as keepsakes and documents) at the back of the higher, less accessible shelves. Next, add the containers that hold seasonal items, such as winter clothing or Christmas decorations. In the most easily accessible area, place containers that hold items you use every month or so, such as gardening equipment and tools.

Downsize Your Ride

There's something else in your garage that you may want to consider getting rid of if you're serious about downsizing. That's your car. It's true that for most of us, owning a car is a given. We depend on it to get to work, head to the movies, or pick up groceries. But as we get older, our needs change. That means our habits should, as well. Perhaps it's time to reevaluate our assumption that every driver in our home needs his or her own vehicle—especially if we've hit retirement age.

If you have more than one car, ask yourself, "Is this a necessity or simply a convenience?" Mull over the practicality, and cost-saving benefits, of car-pooling to work or church, or even to do errands. Perhaps it's time to pass down a vehicle to an adult child or grandchild or to donate it to charity for a tax deduction. If you happen to own an oversized gas guzzler, or an older car that is no longer reliable, you may want to sell it or trade it in for something smaller and more dependable. If you do, purchasing a used car that is more than five years old is the wisest deal financially, because you're beyond the period where a new car depreciates most in value.

If you're downsizing to a retirement community, check out public transportation nearby. Some communities even have complimentary shuttles that can transport you to doctor's appointments and the grocery store. If you only use your car a couple of times a month, weigh the cost of maintaining it year-round with the cost of using a taxi or rideshare company for those occasional outings.

To get a clearer picture of what you REALLY spend over the course of a year to maintain your vehicle, take a few moments to fill out this Downsize Your Ride Worksheet. Is owning this vehicle(s) getting you where you want to go in terms of your Think Small Vision Statement?

EXPENSES

_____ Car Payment
_____ Principal
_____ Interest
_____ Auto Insurance
_____ License and Registration
_____ Maintenance (oil change, tires, etc.)
_____ Repairs
_____ Fuel
_____ Car Washes
_____ Automobile club or emergency service
_____ Garage (additional apartment or condo fee)

_____ TOTAL

Check This Out A car can easily become a mobile closet, if you let it. Receipts, fast food containers, extra jackets, and boxes of items intended for donation, can end up riding around in your car season after season. Why not take a few moments right now to check under the seats, in the side door compartments, the glove box, and the trunk of your car? Apply the Keep, Give Away, Discard method to anything you find.

Garage Sale Guru

If cleaning out the garage inspires you to hold a garage sale, remember: planning precedes haggling. Garage sales can be a lot of work. To make a sale financially worth your time and effort, here are a few tips:

- Before you start making signs and pricing odds and ends, check with city hall or the county clerk's office to see if you need a permit or license to hold a private sale. If you have an HOA, make sure a sale is allowed by its covenants. If a sale at your home isn't a possibility, consider joining together with a friend for a multi-family sale. Not only will you have more goodies to sell, you're likely to have more fun while you're doing it.

- Contact neighbors to see if any of them are interested in holding garage sales on the same day. A neighbor-hood sale is a bigger draw for potential buyers.

- If the thought of selling everything you want to get rid of at one time is overwhelming, consider doing several smaller, themed garage sales. For instance, advertise a Couch Potato Sale, where you only sell items used for entertainment, such as DVDs, video games, electronics, books, games, that old popcorn maker, and (of course) your castoff couch.

- If it's the middle of winter and you want to hold off on your sale until more pleasant weather heads your way, group similarly priced items together in boxes to store until you're ready.

- Instead of recycling grocery bags at the store, start saving them to offer your customers at sale.

- Remember to advertise with flyers and on social media groups and garage sale sites.

- If you have a lot of big-ticket items, consider downloading an app on your tablet or mobile device that allows you to accept credit and debit cards. There's a small fee to use apps like this, but they will allow buyers who do not have cash on hand to make larger purchases. Also, know where the closest ATM is, so you can direct buyers if they'd rather pay cash.

- Play it safe. Don't let anyone you don't know enter your house to use your restroom.

- Sell expensive jewelry, collector's items, or antiques through a reputable online sales site, jeweler, antiques dealer, or "estate" sale, instead of at a garage sale, where there can be a greater chance of theft or being swindled out of something valuable. (Avoid pawn shops, where you'll only receive about 10% of an item's value.)

- Keep an eye on your cash at all times. You may want to wear an apron where you can keep zippered pouches that hold coins and bills separately. That way your money is concealed, but close at hand.

- Always have a friend or family member help you with the sale. You'll need someone to be there in case you need a bathroom break or to deposit cash safely inside on a regular basis, so you don't keep too much money on hand.

- Use different colored sticker dots to price your items. Have several large signs with the key plainly visible. For instance, a green dot means $1, a red dot is $2, and a blue dot is $5. Use white stickers with a written price for larger ticket items.

- Check inside anything with a lid or a pocket for spare change or forgotten items before putting it out for sale.

- Group items in laundry baskets or boxes the night before in your garage to save time setting up in the morning.

- Remember, the more organized your items are, the easier it is for customers to shop—and buy! Make use of card tables, shelves, milk crates, and garment racks. And don't forget to have a chair you can sit on during lulls in the action.

- Display breakables on a sturdy table backed up against a wall or fence, where there is less chance of someone bumping into it and valuables getting broken.

- Have a working extension cord available for customers to try out small appliances.

- Place bigger ticket items near the street to draw customers in.

- Price items at about 10 to 25% of their retail value.

- Make grab bags for $1. Put small toys and odds and ends that are useful, but inexpensive, together. You may want to make special grab bags for kids, if you are selling children's items.

- Before the sale, plan what you're going to do with items that don't sell. If you're going to donate them, arrange the charity to pick up the items shortly after the sale is finished.

Trash or Treasure

What's the difference between an heirloom and a thrift store castoff? Only your heart knows for sure! When memory is attached to the things you own, it's tough to consider downsizing them out of your life. If it's an item that has been passed down from a loved one, or a gift you received that you feel obligated to keep, it can be very difficult to separate practicality from emotion.

In Sweden, some people keep a fulskåp, which is translated as a "cabinet for the ugly." This is where they hide those ceramic cat cookie jars, handknit Christmas sweaters, and knickknacks that are good for a laugh, but nothing more. Then, when the friend or relative who has bestowed this thoughtful (yet impractical or unwanted) gift drops by, they display it somewhere the giver will notice it. Yes, this may sound like a form of kindness. However, it's not only dishonest, it encourages the giver to continue providing tacky little trinkets in the name of love.

Stop the clutter before it starts! Express clearly, but kindly, that you appreciate the generosity of your gift-giving friends but explain that you no longer have room to keep everything you receive. A gift is not an obligation. You do not have to read a book you've been given. You do not have to wear clothing that's been handed down to you. You do not even have to eat that jar of homemade quince jam you receive every year at Christmas. Be appreciative, yet honest—or donate and re-gift.

You also need to be honest with yourself. Do the gifts you give inspire others to start their own fulskåp? This year put more thought and less clutter into the lives of those you love. Instead of feeling pressured to find just the right "thing" for Christmas, birthdays, hostess gifts, and special celebrations, think outside the gift box.

On the next page are a few gracious gift giving ideas that won't end up in the fulskåp:

- Give something edible (homemade or purchased with your own hard–earned cash) that you know the recipient will enjoy eating. You can even whip up a meal that can be frozen and enjoyed at some date when time is at a premium. (Home-made soup is nutritious, easy-to-make, and freezes well).

- Gift cards always fit just right. Show a little extra love, and thought, by wrapping them in a unique way. For instance, put a grocery store gift card inside a mason jar filled with dried beans and a soup recipe. Put a restaurant gift card in a leftover jewelry bag or box and include a copy of the menu.

- Give of your time, instead of your money. Make your own personalized coupon booklet with coupons for much appreciated services, such as babysitting, housecleaning, cooking a meal, running errands, etc.

- Make a donation to your loved one's favorite charity in their name. You can also "buy" gifts on charity sites for those in need around the world. Everything from a flock of chickens to clean water to medical procedures or educational supplies can be purchased as a gift. These usually come with a card or certificate for the recipient and are often tax deductible.

- Name a star in someone's honor through NASA.

- Adopt an animal through your local zoo or a wildlife organization. Your donation will help with preservation and conservation in the name of someone you love. If a building program is in place, you can often purchase a personalized tile with a name or wish on it that you and your loved ones can visit for years to come.

- Give experiences, instead of stuff. Pamper those you love with gift certificates for anything from house cleaning to a car wash, pedicure, or sky diving adventure. Or how about a family membership to the zoo, aquarium, local theme park, or museum?

- Let your creative juices flow! Write a poem or song, or simply a heartfelt note, telling others what you appreciate about them. A sincere "I love you" is always worth more than something new to dust.

- Instead of waiting to pass on heirlooms to your children, do it now. Or, if there is an item you own that a friend has always admired, why not surprise that person by giving it to them for their next birthday?

Holding Onto the Past

Where family heirlooms are concerned, it's easy to confuse their sentimental value with their worth. Some items that are passed down to us are true antiques. Others are just plain old junk with memories attached. If a keepsake's beauty is found in the eye—and heart—of the beholder, how do we determine when to let it go?

Downsizing heirlooms is the same as downsizing a closet, only with more emotional strings attached. We may not even realize how attached they are until we consider getting rid of that oversized dining room table that our parents purchased when they first got married or that odd lamp held together by seashells and glitter that Grandma Gertie brought back from her trip to Boca. While there's nothing wrong with surrounding ourselves with items that remind us of those we love, our home is not a museum. Nor is it a proving ground for displaying our devotion to those who've gone before us.

Things are just things. We may cling to them like we did our security blanket as kids, a blanket that comforted us when we were scared, soothed us when we were hurting, and made us feel at home whenever we held it near. But we're all grown up now. That doesn't mean letting go of family keepsakes will be easy. But it does mean we are mature enough to honor the memories of those we love without sabotaging our downsizing goals.

Be honest with yourself. Is the joy this item gives you found solely in the memories it holds? Would you still like the item if it was not bound up with heartstrings? Will you use it? Will you display it? Will you store it somewhere you'll never even think about it until you move again? Do you hesitate to let go of this item because of its monetary value?

If the heirloom you're holding only gives you joy because it's valuable monetarily, perhaps you should consider if that money would be better spent by, well…being spent. If that antique doll you've inherited, or that vintage iron garden chair that's so uncomfortable no one ever sits in it, is actually worth a good chunk of change, get it appraised by a professional. Then, sell it. Put the proceeds toward reducing debt, invest it, save it, or donate it.

Of course, family heirlooms may also come with family ties to the living. Trying to explain to your siblings why you're "cashing in" on Mom's old mink coat may be harder than choosing to let go of it in the first place. If an estate has been divided among surviving family members, and you would rather liquidate what you've inherited than display it, dust it, or store it until the time comes for you to pass it on to the next generation, allow other family members to purchase the item in question from you.

Money can be a divisive topic. Financial disagreements can open a crack that eventually severs a relationship. Is it worth it? Only you can determine what you can, and can't, live with. While people are always more valuable than possessions, simply handing something over to squelch a disagreement can also plant a seed of resentment within you that only grows stronger as the years go by. Every situation is as unique as the participants in it, as is every family.

The State of the Estate

Dealing with a loved one's estate is understandably stressful. However, there are six scenarios that can make it even more so, sometimes sparking disagreements that continue for years. If any of these situations apply to you, it's best to try to untangle knotted family ties before grief adds fuel to the emotional fire.

1) If sibling rivalry is already present.

2) If the financial situations of siblings are imbalanced, those with fewer financial resources may feel entitled to a larger share of the estate.

3) If one person carries a larger share of the caregiving responsibilities during a parent(s)' latter years, he or she may feel entitled to a larger share of the estate, particularly if the sacrifices he or she has made haven't been acknowledged or adequately "appreciated" by the rest of the family.

4) If the family is blended, or if any members of the family are estranged or have been cut out of the will.

5) If a parent married later in life, children may resent the "new" spouse having an equal share in the estate.

6) If parents have gifted or loaned a sum of money, or given an advanced payout from their estate, to one child, and these financial arrangements are not reflected in their current will.

All of these scenarios can be tricky, especially when emotions are running high. Although talking with aging parents about the details of their estate may be uncomfortable, an honest discussion now may help prevent deeper misunderstandings and hurt feelings later. If your parents are not open to a conversation of this kind, try to have an honest discussion with siblings and other relatives about their expectations concerning your parents' estate. Not every problem can be averted, and not every personality will be amenable. All you can do is your best—that includes applying the lessons you learn to your own estate, to make things as trouble-free for your own heirs as possible.

Downsizing a Home That Isn't Your Own

Downsizing the home of an aging parent or relative is not only a big job, but one fraught with emotional landmines. If you're handling this job while your parent is still alive—and not wholly onboard with the idea—it can be difficult physically, logistically, and relationally, as well as emotionally.

Trying to honor your parents' wishes, while doing what you believe is in their best interest, may not always be possible at the same time. No matter how hard you try. If you have siblings, trying to work together, supporting each other, and providing a united front is key. There are also many service organizations and professionals that can help you better navigate your own place in the next season of your parent's life/ Search online and with community service organizations for these resources.

But the best of intentions and an abundance of resources are still not enough to guarantee a smooth transition. So, how do you know when it's worth fighting for?

Here are six non-negotiables, when it comes to loving your parents well:

1) **SAFETY** As we age, it's harder to maintain our balance, to multitask, and to react quickly. If parents begin to exhibit cuts and bruises, they may be falling or stumbling into things when you're not around. If unexplained dents appear on their car, their eyesight, depth perception, mental faculties, or reaction time may have deteriorated to the point that driving is no longer safe. Don't neglect having a difficult conversation, or taking action, when your parents' safety is on the line.

2) **HEALTH** Old age is a condition that doesn't improve with time. If your parents are no longer able to adequately care for their own changing health issues, it's time to get them the help they need. This may include assistance with tasks such as taking the proper medication at the proper time, administering insulin shots (if necessary), avoiding bedsores and pressure ulcers by regularly getting out of the recliner, or staying on a special diet.

3) **MEALS** Good health depends on good nutrition. If your parents appear to be losing weight, having difficulty getting to the grocery store, or if there is a large amount of spoiled food in their fridge—or left on the counter, it's time to make certain their nutritional needs are being met.

4) **HOUSEKEEPING** Not everyone is a neat freak. However, if your parents' housekeeping has declined below their usual standards, it needs to be addressed. If their dishes and laundry are piling up, if trash isn't making it out to the curb for pick up, if cobwebs are appearing in random corners, and you find yourself cutting a visit short just so you don't have to use their bathroom, helping them do a thorough clean every now and then may be well intentioned, but it isn't sufficient. They need regular visits from a bonded, licensed, and insured cleaning service—or it's time to discuss moving to a smaller, more manageable home, preferably a senior living facility with varying cares of assistance available.

5) **HYGIENE** If your parents begin to smell "funny," don't just chalk it up to old age. They may have stopped showering because it's too difficult for them or they may be worried about falling in the shower. If their clothing is soiled, they may struggle to manage doing laundry—or they may no longer notice or care about their appearance. Any or all of the above are not only unpleasant for all of those involved, they can also adversely affect your parents' health and social life.

6) **COMMUNITY** Having a social life that's broader than dining in front of the television or posting memes on social media is not a luxury for aging parents. It's a necessity. Be sure your aging parent has plenty of "real time" with neighbors, family members, church and social groups.

To Each His Own

Dividing up the assets of an estate between beneficiaries can sound rather cold and impersonal but dealing with a loved one's possessions never is. If there is more than one heir, figuring out who gets what is more than dividing up equal slices of a financial pie. It's a tricky dance of give-and-take.

Here are three ways that can help you avoid stepping on anyone's toes as you move forward:

1) Give each heir a pad of sticky notes, each a different color. Take turns beginning with the oldest, or the one who's had the greatest caregiving responsibility, putting a sticky note on an item you would like.

2) Number each item. Ask everyone to list the numbers of items they would like. If two or more people list the same item, draw straws to see who will receive it.

3) Put a monetary value on each item. Add up the total of all of the items and divide that amount between the number of heirs. Each heir gets to "spend" their designated amount of money on whichever items they would like. If more than one person wants an item, they can "bid" for it.

4) If heirs are not able to participate in dividing the estate in person, include them through a video call.

5) Use this time for family reminiscing. Talk about the items you're choosing, what they mean to you and why.

6) If there are items no one wants, don't feel guilted into "adopting" them into your home. Just because something holds special meaning doesn't mean you have to hold onto it. Save a photo of the item. Write about it in your journal. Pass on stories to your kids and grandkids about what it means to you. If it's a piece of clothing, like a wedding gown, or a holiday tablecloth or Christmas tree skirt that isn't in good shape, take a swatch of fabric and frame it along with a family photo.

Check This Out

If you're serious about keeping your own clutter under control, choose wisely when it comes to taking on what was once someone else's possessions. Something small can be just as meaningful as something large, so Think Small. Take one tea cup or silver spoon, instead of an entire tea set or case of silverware. If you would need to mail or ship an item, consider whether it is worth the cost. Ask yourself where the item will reside in your home. If you can't think of any place it will go other than storing it in the garage, basement, or attic, perhaps it isn't something you need to bring home with you after all.

Guarding History

Along with the cookie jars and credenzas, dividing an estate may also involve deciding what to do with items such as family records, love letters, journals, military medals, awards, and photos. Designate a "family historian" (preferably someone with ample storage space) who will be responsible for legal documents, such as birth certificates, marriage licenses, and immigration documents. First, scan these documents to retain a digital copy. Then, store them in an archival quality file box, preferably in a home safe or safety deposit box. This way they are safe from fire, flood, heat, and bugs.

For those items you DO want to store for posterity, make sure you have stored them properly. There's nothing worse than taking up space for a box filled with "history" only to open it one day and find a moth-eaten wedding dress, old candles melted onto wedding photos, and love poems reduced to bits of brittle, unreadable, yellowed paper scraps.

If you're using plastic tubs, choose opaque (not clear) polypropylene or polyethylene containers. Prepare it for duty by cleaning it with rubbing alcohol and letting it dry. Only use acid-free plastic, or archival plastic sleeves, for storing photos, CDs or DVDs containing family photos, collectible cards, or stamps. Store it somewhere dark, free from moisture and excessive heat.

When it comes to old love letters and journals, it's tempting to want to save everything your parents possessed to try to gain a better picture of your own history. However, unless you are going to write a biography or delve more deeply into your family tree than you can do through genealogy sites, let them go. They will most likely deteriorate to the point of becoming unreadable over time. If your interest is peaked, read through them once, scan any pages that are of true interest, and recycle the rest.

If you're going through a loved one's old photos ditch the landscape photos. Throw out any unflattering photos of your loved ones, unless it's so unflattering that it's likely to become a family favorite! If you don't know the people in a photo, and their identity is of interest to you, scan it and email it to older members of the family, asking for any information they may have. Carefully write people's names on the back of photos, using a photo safe archival pen. Choose your favorites carefully. You don't need three angles of the same shot.

Once you've chosen your favorites, frame them, put them in a photo safe album, or scan them (saving them onto a disc or photo thumb drive). When time allows, you can turn your scanned photos into albums, pillows, blankets, mugs, puzzles—or countless other items—using one of the many photo sites online.

Photo Finish

Sorting through the photos of a loved one can be daunting. But, so can downsizing your own photo stash! When photos switched from film to digital, it was definitely a mixed blessing. Yes, it made photography more affordable, accessible, and convenient. We no longer have to spend money on film, wait days to see whether or not the pics of the grandkids turned out, or even have a camera on hand to snap the perfect shot. All we need is our phone. And if we don't like what we see, we can immediately delete it, take another shot, or tweak the original using photo editing software.

The problem is that all of this makes it easier than ever to become a photo hoarder. Instead of bookshelves filled with photo albums or envelopes filled with prints, we now have phones, computers, and the cloud to fill with our images. That means when we try to show someone a photo of our daughter's graduation, we may first have to scroll through her baby pictures!

Taking a photo and using a photo are two different things. While there's some satisfaction in simply capturing an image of a moment that's significant to us, having thousands of digital photos that we do nothing with—or that hinder us from finding the one photo that we're searching for—is a waste of time and cyberspace.

So, let's cut down on photo hoarding. Here's how to get started:

- **If you take a photo solely for social media, to text to a friend, or to document something (like damage to your car from a hail storm), as soon as you use it, DELETE it.**

- **If you take multiple shots of the same image, save your favorite and DELETE the rest.**

- **Think before you click. You can enjoy your granddaughter's first steps, or your plate of sushi, without taking time away from the actual experience to document it—especially if the only reason you're taking a photo is to share it on social media.**

- When you go on vacation, take some time each day to edit the photos you've taken. Save a vertical and a horizontal shot of your favorites to use for a photo book. DELETE the rest.

- If you find yourself taking out your phone to take a photo simply because everyone around you is doing so, rethink your actions. Is looking at the ocean waves, or watching the jellyfish in the aquarium or the juggler at the park, all you really want and need?

- After ruthlessly editing your vacation photos down, create a slideshow for friends and relatives. Add royalty free music, keep it under 15 minutes, save it onto a CD. Save your original photos onto a thumb drive, in case you'd like to print any photos at a later date. Then DELETE the photos from your phone or computer.

- Learn how to use your photo editing software on your computer. Organize your photos by date, place, or person. Take the time to "tag" people in photos. Then, if you're searching for a specific photo of someone, you can bring up all of the photos you have of that individual by name.

- Always set the time and date feature on your camera. Then, if you download vacation photos from your phone, as well as a camera, they will be grouped together by the day they are taken. This makes it easier to track down a specific shot.

- Use your photos. Make albums, have your favorites images printed and switch outdated framed photos with more recent shots. Scan old photos and combine them with recent photos to make family albums, story books for grandkids, or cookbooks filled with your family's favorite recipes.

- If you still have a stash of negatives or slides, you can pay to have a service scan or digitalize these images, or you can purchase your own equipment to do the job relatively inexpensively. If you continue to store them away in a garage, crawlspace, or attic, these images may be lost due to moisture or heat, unless you store them with care.

Collectible or Clutter?

Photos aren't the only things we collect over time. Some of us started collecting baseball cards, postage stamps, or comic books when we were just kids. As we grew older, we may have added vintage postcards, antique dolls, or memorabilia from our favorite band. Or perhaps we have a penchant for pigs. Or hedgehogs. Or anything bearing an image of the Eiffel Tower. Whatever our collectible of choice, when it's time to downsize, it's time to reevaluate the tchotchkes, gewgaws, and doohickeys that we hold onto "just because."

It's fun to collect stuff. Over time, it becomes part of our identity. It gives us something to search for on vacation or at the mall. It gives other people gift ideas for birthdays and special celebrations. Once it's known we have a "thing" for, say... narwhals, we're liable to wind up with mugs, magnets, slippers, and snow globes, all bearing an image of our beloved unicorn of the sea. So, when should we say "when"?

Collectibles collect dust and take up space. They also cost money. Some people try to rationalize their cute little clutter addiction by assuring themselves that their treasures will be worth something someday, if they just hold onto them long enough. But times have changed. The reason a collectible increases in value is because it is rare and highly desired. However, the internet has made it easier to find, and acquire, everything our hearts desire. The items we used to spend hours searching antique shops, garage sales, and flea markets for can now be found in a matter of minutes online. This has driven their price down.

Even the market for fine art is showing signs of slowing down. While we may not own an original Picasso, we may be holding onto artwork that we've had for years. This should lead us to ask ourselves, if the value that art, antiques, and collectibles hold is really measured by how much they are worth to us.

- Why am I holding onto this? Really?

- Does this help make my home feel more like my own?

- Does this bestow joy every time I look at it?

- Does this match my current décor?

- Does this fit comfortably into the space available in my home?

- Would I purchase this same thing today? If not, why not?

- If this treasure is stored away, instead of on display, is it honestly worth keeping it?

Coins that you don't spend, stamps that you never send, commemorative plates that reside on the wall instead of at the dinner table, or collectible spoons that never touch soup or ice cream, may be stuff you simply don't need to continue taking responsibility for. However, if you've had them for a long time, it may be hard to let them go.

Take a little time to write about your artwork and collectibles in the space below. List each item you use solely for display, or that you have stored away, that has no true use other than to make your home pretty and your heart happy. That is not a bad purpose! Just take a little time and thought re-evaluating whether these items should continue residence in your house or whether it's time they found a new home.

_____

_____

_____

_____

_____

_____

_____

What's Hiding Under Your Sink?

Okay, it's time to come back inside from the garage and down from the attic, so we can continue downsizing the rest of our home. Where to next? Let's start with something relatively small—the bathroom.

"Piece of cake!" you think. Other than a bath towel and an extra roll of toilet paper, there's not much there. Or is there? If you start downsizing your bathroom the same way you did your bedroom closet, you may see things differently in a matter of minutes. Just because it's hidden, doesn't mean it isn't hoarding.

Take everything out, including what's in your bathtub or shower, in your medicine cabinet, in drawers, on shelves, and under the sink. Organize it into separate piles, such as hair care products, make-up, medications, and first aid. Then, work your way through one pile at a time. Here are a few tips to help you whittle down what you find:

LINENS

- Keep two bath towels and washcloths per person; one to use while the other is in the laundry.

- Keep two to four hand towels per bathroom, depending on how often you do the laundry.

- Keep a couple of extra towels and washcloths for guests.

- Keep one bathmat for each bathroom, with a spare for when one is in the laundry.

- Any towel that is frayed or discolored, cut into rags to use for cleaning.

- Any towels that are still in good condition, but more than you need or use, donate to charities, such as homeless shelters or second-hand charitable stores.

- If you use loofahs or sponges in the bath, dispose of loofahs every three weeks and sponges every seven.

SHAMPOO AND TOILETRIES

- Ask yourself, "Do I use this?" not "Might I use this one day?"

- Refuse to stock up on shampoos and lotions when they're on sale. Have only one back-up bottle at a time. If you buy a large economy size bottle, use it to fill a smaller bottle for daily use. Store the larger refills in a linen closet, pantry, or laundry room— IF you have room.

- Don't fill your suitcase with travel-sized toiletries from hotels just because they're "free." Only keep on hand what you will use traveling, or for your guests, over the next year. Donate any additional bottles to local shelters.

- Toss anything that changes in smell, texture, or color. Expired toiletries usually just lose their effectiveness over time, but sometimes they can lead to skin irritation. Here are the recommended expiration dates for common toiletries:

  ~ Shampoo, conditioner, and hair styling products: 1–2 years opened, 3 years unopened
  ~ Shaving cream and toothpaste: 2 years
  ~ Mouthwash: 3 years from manufacture date, which is found on the label
  ~ Deodorant: 3 years
  ~ Soap, both bar and liquid: 3 years
  ~ Sunscreen: 1 year

MEDICATIONS

- You can dispose of medication in the trash by mixing it with dirt, kitty litter, or used coffee grounds, then placing it in a sealable plastic bag. If the medication is prescription, be sure to scratch out any personal information on the bottle before throwing away the container.

- You can also take expired, unused, or unwanted medication to a Safe Medication Disposal kiosk at your local pharmacy.

- Do not flush expired or unused medications down the toilet. It can affect the purity of our drinking water, as well as wind up in lakes and streams, where it can harm wildlife.

FIRST AID

- Although what you keep in your first aid kit will vary depending on the age and needs of those living in your home, here is a list of basics it's always good to have on hand:

  - ~ Up-to-date first-aid manual
  - ~ Adhesive bandages in different sizes and shapes
  - ~ Nonstick sterile bandages
  - ~ Roll of gauze
  - ~ Adhesive tape
  - ~ Antibiotic ointment
  - ~ Antiseptic wipes
  - ~ Thermometer
  - ~ Hydrogen peroxide for disinfectant
  - ~ Aloe vera gel
  - ~ Anti-diarrhea medication
  - ~ Scissors and tweezers
  - ~ Hydrocortisone cream for rashes
  - ~ Eyewash solution
  - ~ Antihistamine

- Your first aid kit is only as useful as the effectiveness of what you have inside. Be sure to keep your medications, as well as your list of emergency contact numbers up to date.

- Keep your first aid kit (as well as all medications), out of the reach of children—but easily accessible to you.

MAKE-UP

- Expired or unwanted cosmetics are just as hazardous to wash into our water supply as unused medications. Although you can throw them into the trash, there is a current movement to keep old cosmetics out of landfills. Several upscale cosmetic manufacturers offer reward programs for turning in unwanted cosmetics. There are also recycling programs available online. You can also drop them off at your local HHW (Household Hazardous Waste) facility.

- Remember to store cosmetics away from heat, humidity, and sunlight.

- While it can be fun to try out new cosmetics, they can expire rather quickly, particularly if you don't use them often. After they expire, they can irritate your skin and eyes. So, purchase frugally and toss regularly. Here are guidelines on expiration dates for common cosmetics:

  - ~ Mascara: 4–6 months
  - ~ Moisturizers, skin creams, and eye creams: 1 year (6–9 months for anything in a jar)
  - ~ Concealer: 1 year
  - ~ Foundation: oil-based, 18 months; water-based, 12 months
  - ~ Powder: 2 years
  - ~ Lipstick: 2–3 years
  - ~ Nail polish: 2–3 years
  - ~ Eye shadow: 3 years
  - ~ Eye and lip pencils: 3–5 years
  - ~ Perfume: 3–5 years

Once you've sorted through your bathroom piles and determined what to Keep, what to Give Away, and what to Discard, give all of your storage area a thorough cleaning before reorganizing. Save space, clean up clutter, and aid accessibility with these handy ideas:

- Use plastic vanity dividers for organizing cosmetics in drawers.

- Use plastic "lazy susans" under your sink for easy access to hair care or cleaning products.

- If your drawer space is limited, consider using plastic caddies. Put everything you need for your morning routine in one caddy and everything you need for the evening in another. Or have one caddy for you and one for your spouse. Put your caddy on the counter for use and then back under the sink when you're finished. Poof! Clean, clutter-free countertops.

- Hang towels from hooks, instead of towel bars, to save space. Or use antique doorknobs to add a funky vibe to your bathroom décor.

- If you have a small shower, and nowhere to keep your shampoo, etc., place a second shower rod inside your shower near the wall. Using rust-resistant hooks, hang loofahs, shower caps, glass door squeegee and/or a plastic caddy to hold your shower essentials.

- Place a tension rod under your sink. Hang cleaning products on the rod by their spray spouts. This makes bottles easily visible and uses vertical space, saving you a bit of space beneath them for rags, back-up bottles of hand soap, etc.

- Make certain your bathroom décor is moisture-proof. Do not display photos or fine artwork anywhere near a shower.

- Put an adhesive magnetic strip on the inside of your medicine cabinet door. Use it to keep tweezers, manicure scissors, eyelash curler, bobby pins and metal barrettes, etc.

- Whether you decide your bathroom scale is essential—or discardable— is totally up to you!

GIVE YOURSELF A BREAK

Downsizing is work, physically, mentally, and emotionally. If you've made it this far in this book by doing more than simply reading, it's time you gave yourself a Day Off. Everyone needs one. While the aim of downsizing is to reduce clutter, responsibility, and the stress that too much stuff can add to your life, the true goal is to make the most of life itself. Learning to think small, allows you to live big!

Consider downsizing as diet and exercise for your lifestyle. Your home will hopefully look trimmer and more attractive in the end, but the ultimate hope is that YOU will feel happier and healthier.

As we all know, getting in shape doesn't happen overnight. It takes time, determination, hard work, and a bit of sacrifice. But somedays, we just want a piece of cake. It doesn't mean we've fallen off the wagon. It doesn't mean we've failed. It doesn't mean we'll never be the size we want. It simply means that today, we're going to sit back and celebrate how far we've come. Tomorrow, we'll get back to work.

Taking a day off doesn't mean throwing our clothes all over the floor or maxing out our credit card buying new junk to replace the old junk we worked so hard to get rid of. That may feel like a treat—for a moment or two. But it won't refresh us. Eventually, we'll have to pick up the clothes, pay the bill, and take care of the stuff we purchased. It's like preemptive procrastination. We're simply putting off the consequences of poor choices until later. Instead, think about what truly refreshes you. What leaves you feeling better after you've done it, without any unpleasant consequences? A walk in the woods? Reading a magazine in a comfy chair? Spending the whole day focused on your favorite craft or hobby? Lunch out with a friend? Taking your grandkids to the zoo?

If this question leaves you stumped, it's time you refreshed your memory, as well as your spirit. Think about your most memorable days. What made them resonate so deeply with you? Take the seed of what you enjoyed most and plant it in some new experiences.

To help you get started, list ten things that energize you, refresh you, and give you joy.

1. _____

2. _____

3. _____

4. _____

5. _____

6. _____

7. _____

8. _____

9. _____

10. _____

Do one of these ten things today! Don't just settle for becoming clutter-free. Strive to become joy-filled!

KITCHEN AID

Now that you're refreshed, you're ready to tackle one of the most clutter-prone parts of your home: the kitchen. Unless you eat out every day, your kitchen is bound to be a hub of activity, with a strong potential for organizational chaos.

For some people, their kitchen is like a craft room—only with better snacks. Preparing meals is an act of love and creativity. It's a gift they give, a way to care for others in a tangible way. Sure, some days they may order pizza, but if they had the time, money, and energy, they'd prefer to whip up something delicious on their own. Perhaps something they've seen on one of those cooking shows they love to watch. They love their gadgets, everything from their avocado slicer and cherry pitter, to their herb stripper and mushroom brush.

For others, the kitchen is merely a means to an end. People have got to eat, and this is where the microwave resides. For them, grocery shopping is a necessary evil and the fridge is always well-stocked with frozen dinners. Don't ask them which knife is best for slicing bread. Their answer will always be, "Whichever is close at hand."

Which camp you lean more towards will greatly influence how big of a challenge it will be to downsize your kitchen. If you're a foodie, don't get discouraged or feel tempted to skip this part and move on to the next room! You don't have to give up your egg slicer. You simply need to treat it like you did the clothes in your closet. Ask yourself:

- Do I use this regularly?

- Just because I used this a lot in the past, does it still fit the way I cook today? (Perhaps it's time to say adieu to that deep fryer, bread box, or hand mixer.)

- Do I have multiples of this? (Whether you're holding onto 10 spatulas or 10 pair of jeans, some are rarely going to be used.)

- Is there anything I'm keeping for emotional reasons? (Yes, you can become emotionally attached to a gelatin mold you inherited from your mother.)

- Do I have room for this in my kitchen?

- Am I keeping this because I like the idea of using it or will I actually use it? (If you've held onto that sushi rolling mat for three years, but never used it, give in to the fact that perhaps you only want to order sushi, not make it at home.)

The kitchen is one room where it's best to refrain from taking everything out and putting it into a pile. There'd simply be way too much stuff! Not only that, if you did pile it all on the floor, you'd have to rewash before you put it away. Besides, the ice cream would get way too soft!

It's best to downsize your kitchen by breaking it down into different areas and tackling them one at a time, beginning with the Big Four: drawers, cabinets, pantry, and refrigerator. Each of these can then be broken down into smaller categories, such as dinnerware, pots and pans, and cooking gadgets, or frozen foods and refrigerated foods. Doing this is as much of a mental game as it is a practical plan. Give yourself goals that you can accomplish in an hour or so. That way, you don't tire out before you finish—or have to stop to get dinner ready with half of your utensils still strewn all over the kitchen counter.

It's up to you to choose where to start. If you're up to the challenge, begin with the area that drives you the craziest. The sense of accomplishment you'll have when you're done may encourage you to jump right into tackling another area. As you work your way through the kitchen, use the tips on the next page to help you downsize and organize each area.

DRAWERS

This is not only where your flatware finds a home, but where most of those little kitchen gadgets take up residence. It's easy for items to land here and never again see the light of day, until you pack them up to move to a new address. How many times have you assured yourself that you know you have a soup ladle, but had to go through several drawers, multiple times, before you actually laid your hands on it? Without an organizational plan, kitchen drawers can become vast caverns where you repeatedly find yourself searching for the right sized measuring spoon amidst potato peelers, wire whisks, loose bamboo skewers, random cutlery, and packages of chopsticks from your favorite Asian restaurant.

However, before you start to organize, you need to downsize. Begin with your flatware drawer. For most people, this is usually the most organized drawer in their kitchen, thanks to a flatware divider. If you don't have one, now's the time to commit! The less time you spend searching for a soup spoon, the more time you'll have to search for your car keys!

Count how many complete five-piece place settings you have. Are you short on spoons? Do you care if your serving pieces don't match? (Some people find that look eclectically appealing, while others view it as tacky!) Knowing you only have five knives when you are having six guests over for dinner will prevent you from searching every drawer looking for another knife. Better yet, after purging your kitchen, find replacements for the items that are broken or missing. Stop searching for what you don't have or trying to use what won't work.

Next, move on to the Keep, Give Away, Discard, or Sell phase. Get rid of any random pieces of flatware from old sets you no longer use. Consider how many place settings you realistically need. Scrutinize your serving pieces. Do you really need three gravy ladles?

If you have a set of real silver, as opposed to stainless steel flatware, take time to consider whether this truly is an item that gives you joy! Good silver flatware is usually used only once or twice a year for special occasions. It must be polished with a jewelry polishing cloth. If you use a chemical tarnish remover, you'll take off the factory finish which will reduce its value. While it can be put in the dishwasher, it needs to be put in a basket separate from your stainless steel flatware. If they touch, the silver can become discolored and pitted. If your fine silver has gold accents, it needs to be washed by hand. True sterling silver can be worth several hundred dollars and easily sold at a jeweler. Would the money be of more use to you than the fancy flatware? (Before you head to a jeweler, make sure the word "sterling" is imprinted on the back. If not, it is silver-plated, which is useful as flatware, but not worth much monetarily.)

Once you've sorted through your flatware, clean out the drawer where you will keep it before returning it to its place. Choose the drawer closest to where you usually eat. If you could use more storage space in your kitchen and are short on drawers, consider getting a small sideboard cabinet in your dining space where you can keep your flatware, dinnerware, placemats, napkins, and party items. It's one way to keep a smaller home more clutter-free.

Next, tackle the rest of the drawers. Empty everything onto a clean table or counter. Sort items by category, such as things used to stir, to cut, to measure, for baking, etc. Whatever designation makes the most sense to you, will help you organize your kitchen in the most practical and convenient way for you. Then, it's time to get ruthless.

- **Whittle down your duplicates. You may need a couple of large spoons for stirring or serving, but do you really need three set of measuring spoons—regardless of how cute they are?**

- **Dispose of anything that is irreparably broken or rusted.**

- **If you have any of these items, ask yourself if you really need them, or if they are simply cluttering up a drawer:**

  ~ **Pasta measurer**
  ~ **Egg slicer**
  ~ **Apple slicer**
  ~ **Avocado slicer**
  ~ **Pie crust shield (use a strip of aluminum foil)**
  ~ **Pastry cutter (use a fork or food processor, instead)**

~ **Cherry pitter (unless you make cherry pies more than once a decade)**
~ **Garlic press (press garlic with the flat side of a knife and give it one big whack. Voila! Instant garlic press.)**
~ **Soft boiled egg cracker**
~ **Egg separator**
~ **Banana slicer**
~ **Meat shredding claws (use two serving forks)**
~ **Corn kernel stripper (a knife works just fine)**
~ **Pie bird (just cut holes in the top of the crust to let steam escape)**
~ **Tuna press**
~ **Taco holder**
~ **Pickle picker**
~ **Burger press**
~ **Escargot tongs**

Once your items are sorted, and your drawers are wiped clean, it's time to put what remains into some semblance of order. That means using expandable drawer dividers or plastic bins to separate your cooking utensils and gadgets. If you put cork, felt, or a grip plastic shelf liner in the drawer, it will keep the bins from moving and rattling around each time you close the drawer. Be as intentional about which drawer you put items in as about what you put in it. Keep items in the drawer closest to where they will be used. For instance, keep pot holders near the stove, cutting boards near the knives, and extra kitchen towels near the sink.

Don't forget the drawer under your oven! Although it can be used as a "warming drawer" where you keep dishes warm until everything makes it to the dinner table, it's better put to use as a storage space for large, bulky items, such as cookie sheets, sheet pans, and skillets. Just remember to wipe it out frequently, since random crumbs, etc., may fall into it as you're putting things in the oven.

Organize items into your drawers using the same groupings that you did to sort them, (such as things to cut, to stir, to measure, etc.). Some people keep a special "chef's drawer" right next to the stove, which contains all of the essentials you use most frequently, such as a pot holder, your most versatile knife, a large spoon and spatula, a set of measuring spoons, etc. The personalized mix is up to you. So is what you choose to keep, how you sort it, where you put it, and how you organize it.

Remember, equally as important as keeping only what you use and storing it somewhere convenient, is always putting items back in the same place. An organized kitchen is one where you can put your hands on what you need right when you need it—without scrambling through random drawers searching for a wooden spoon as your custard is on the brink of boiling over and already sticking to the bottom of your pot.

KNICKKNACK NICHE

There is one drawer that almost every home has that's affectionately known as "the junk drawer." It's where the little odds and ends of life are tossed on the fly. This is the spot where items such as scissors, pens, paper clips, rubber bands, take-out menus, coupons, and random business cards often come to rest.

Having one junk drawer is not a bad thing. It's better than having an entire home that qualifies as one! But now that you're downsizing your life, taking a few moments to sort through that dark hole of novelties is a productive use of your time. Chances are you'll find much of what's in there can be tossed out (e.g. expired coupons, nonrefillable pens that have run out of ink, paper clips bent beyond usefulness). As for the rest, add a few small plastic trays to help organize it. While you're at it, why not change its name? A junk drawer invites you to throw things into it that you don't want to take the time to put away or to decide if they are even worth keeping. Don't keep junk. Only hold onto what's useful. You might even want to add an adhesive bandage and burn ointment, so when a kitchen mishap takes place, you have what you need close at hand.

CABINETS AND SHELVES

On to the BIG stuff! By now, you know what to do. Take everything out, put it on a clean table or counter, and get sorting! Below are a few appliances you may want to carefully consider as to whether they're worth the space they take up in your cabinets—and the time it takes to clean them!

- Any gimmicky TV ad purchase. These cooking gizmos look fun on the commercials but are often more work than they're worth.

- Anything with the word "maker" attached to it, such as a grilled cheese maker, hot dog maker, s'more maker, quesadilla maker, etc. All of these foods can easily be made using your regular pots and pans. Other than a coffee maker or waffle maker, most of these "makers" take up a lot of room in your cabinets and get very limited use.

- Any item that makes fast-and-easy desserts, such as a donut kit, cupcake kit, or ice cream churn. Do you really need a dozen warm donuts in the blink of an eye? If you have a true donut craving, go to a donut shop and buy ONE. Your kitchen cabinets, and your waistline, will thank you.

- A panini press. Use your waffle iron or put one pan on top of the panini sandwich you're grilling in another pan. Poof! Instant, clutter-free panini press.

- Multi-use blenders, juicers, and mixers. Not only do these take up a huge amount of space, and often have lots of additional parts that are hard to keep track of, they can take longer to clean than to use.

- Pizza stone. If you use it often, great. If not, it's cumbersome to store, easily broken, and cannot be washed with soap, which gets into its porous surface—resulting in soapy tasting pizza.

- Crock pot. If the one in your cupboard has been there since your children were small, and it's the size of a hot tub, it may be time to downsize or donate.

- A sous vide circulator, raclette maker, or aebleskiver pan. If you can't spell it or pronounce it, chances are you don't use it and really don't need it.

POTS AND PANS

One good set of pots and pans will last for years, if you care for them. If yours have a nonstick surface, cut old plastic placemats in circles that fit inside the bottom of each pot and pan. Then, you can stack them without scratching them, as well as give older, worn placemats a second life.

Using a hanging pot rack is also a great way to save cabinet space. If you like the look—and have a spot in your kitchen where people won't hit their head on a frying pan—give it a try.

DINNERWARE

How many sets of dishes do you own? How many do you use? How many do you have room for? What about glassware? How many wine glasses do you really need? Do you regularly use all of those loyalty cups from movie theatres and fast food restaurants? Is the space dedicated to storing them worth the $1 you save each six months when you use them—or forget to bring them with you?

The answer to each of these questions will help determine how to sort your dinnerware. As for any fine china or holiday dinnerware, once again, it's a matter of space, use, and emotional ties. Choose what you'll use.

PARTY ACCOUTREMENTS

Whether you love, or loathe, entertaining will obviously help determine how much space you dedicate to storing the odds and ends that only come out when guests arrive. Cake plates, chip and dip sets, tiered serving platters, a chocolate fountain, or crystal punch bowl can take up a lot of space. Also, if you don't use them frequently you not only have to wash them after you use them, but before.

If you're short on space, you can purchase relatively inexpensive, disposable party items when you need them and donate that large Christmas tree-shaped cookie platter to charity. It will free up a good amount of space that you can use year-round.

However, if hospitality is your thing, save space in your kitchen by keeping all of your celebratory items together in a sealable plastic bin in the garage or storage space. Group items together by occasion. Put smaller items, such as candles, leftover party napkins, and party hats together in zip-lock bags. (If you live in an extremely warm climate, keep the candles inside.) Label each bin, stack it, and don't think about it again until it's time to party.

PLASTICWARE

Plasticware lids are the lost socks of the kitchen. Begin downsizing your plastic stash by matching each of your containers to a lid that actually fits. If a container is stained, pitted, or missing a lid, you can often recycle it. Check with your local recycler for guidelines.

Some plasticware companies actually have a lifetime guarantee. Take advantage of it! Better yet, swear off plastic containers and use long-lasting, easily-cleanable, more eco-friendly glass containers.

COOKBOOKS

Looking at cookbooks can be as much fun as actually trying out their recipes. However, times have changed. Do you want to know the all-time best recipe for pot roast? How to use leftover hash browns? The correct amount of time it takes to cook a 23-pound turkey? Yes, your cookbook library may hold the answer, but to find it you have to search through them, page-by-page.

Today, the internet is our fastest, most convenient cookbook. That doesn't mean it's the most aesthetically pleasing. There is still a place for cookbooks, especially for those who read them like coffee table books—for inspiration, education, and vicarious snacking. Even if that describes you, it doesn't mean your library can't use a little downsizing.

Take a look at each cookbook you have on hand. When was the last time you opened it? When was the last time you actually prepared a recipe from it? If there's one recipe you use over and over again, but it's all you use the cookbook for, scan it. Then, donate the cookbook. Either keep a file on your computer, or on a memory stick, that contains your favorite recipes.

If you prefer paper over digital, print a copy of your favorite recipes. Purchase a box of 3-hole-punch plastic sleeves and a binder. Put copies of your favorite recipes, old recipe cards, and recipes clipped from the newspaper or torn out of magazines, inside. Organize the pages by category. One great benefit of this homemade cookbook is that you can remove an individual page when you're using the recipe. Not only that, it's protected from splatters and spills by the plastic sleeve.

Check This Out

If you have a lot of recipes for family favorites or traditional dishes that have been passed down, you can turn them into a useful, memorable gift for Christmas, birthdays, weddings, and graduations. Go to an online website where you can create photo albums. Choose a "storybook" style of album. Type in the recipes and add a few of your favorite family photos. It's a great gift to give to your children when they're ready to leave the nest and strike out living, and cooking, on their own.

SHELF LINERS...TO LINE OR NOT TO LINE?

Lining shelves is a long-held tradition when moving into a new home. But is it necessary—or even helpful? Removing old, gummy adhesive liners often leaves behind a sticky residue, not to mention an assortment of age-old crumbs and bugs. It's true that if items are put away before they're completely dry, shelf liners can keep water spots from forming on wood shelves. However, if your cabinets are laminate, lining your shelves is unnecessary.

If you're a shelf-liner fan, here are a few wise ways to use them:

- **Stay away from adhesive liners. Use cork, plastic grip, or machine washable liners.**

- **If you do use shelf liners, remove all items from your shelves regularly to wash the liners.**

- Adding slightly padded shelf liners can add a quiet, meditative feel to putting away your dishes.

- Always put a shelf liner beneath your sink, preferably one that's easily removable and cleanable.

- If you have open shelving or glass cabinets, lining the back of them with a bright, adhesive shelf liner can add a pleasant pop of color.

- As to whether you should store your glasses upside-down or right-side up, you should store them right side up if you do not have shelf liners, to keep the lips of the glasses clean. If you have shelf liners, you can store them any way you want!

RESURFACE YOUR COUNTERTOPS

Do you have enough room on your kitchen countertops to prepare a meal? Or do you have to push aside yesterday's paper, this morning's dishes, today's mail, an aging blender, and a large ceramic chicken, just to eke out enough space to use your cutting board? If you fall into the latter category, your countertops may need resurfacing. Not with granite or marble, but with a little elbow grease in search of that last frontier…space.

Make sure you USE what's on your counter. The coffee maker you use every morning makes sense. However, the large mixer that you only use once or twice a year for holiday baking might find a better home in the garage or pantry. A knife block is another item that take up a lot of counterspace. Putting your kitchen knives in individual sheathes and keeping them in a drawer near your cutting board not only keeps your knives cleaner, but makes your kitchen look cleaner and less cluttered. You want to have enough open space on your counter to cook—and to place your grocery bags after shopping. If your counter is where you throw your car keys, mail, and whatever happens to be in your hands when you come in from the garage, consider using a small basket to corral it all. This will also keep items from winding up in a random water puddle or grease spot.

Kitchen counters are designed with easily cleanable surfaces. That's because water, grease, flour, tomato sauce, crumbs, and any other foodstuff you can think of, winds up splattered all over them. Whatever is setting on your counter, will inevitably end up wearing a bit of this mess, as well. So, make sure whatever you place there is waterproof and easy to clean.

FOOD—THE HEART OF THE KITCHEN

A century ago, people went to a grocer to purchase dry goods, a butcher for meat, and a greengrocer for their fruits and veggies. They used ice boxes to keep perishables cool, which worked about as well as a stadium cooler. They shopped every day or two, since foods weren't packed full of preservatives and groceries spoiled quickly.

By the 1920s, cooking from scratch fell out of favor and canned goods and ready-to-cook meals came into style. In the 1930s, refrigerators became a common household appliance, which meant that meat, eggs, and dairy could stay fresher longer. By the 40s, frozen foods were the fad. However, as a result of World War II, food rationing changed the way Americans ate from 1942 to 1946. Nothing was wasted. Every morsel was appreciated.

By the 1950s, eating habits changed again. Rationing was out. Choice was in. Now, the neighborhood "grocery" store is also likely to house a florist, bank, bakery, deli, and coffee shop, as well as sell home goods, and even clothing. In other words, downsizing is not something we seem to want our grocery stores to do.

This is wonderful for a cook who likes diversity on the menu, but it's also helped us get into the habit of hoarding and wasting food. According to the F.A.O. (Food and Agriculture Organization), Americans wastes about 40% of the food we buy each year. That's about one pound of food per person, per day. Every time we waste food, we clog landfills, increase greenhouse emissions of methane, and waste water, land, energy—and our money.

Recent surveys revealed the average American family throws out $2,000 worth a food a year. That's a lot of money down the garbage disposal.

When we take all of this into consideration, it looks like our kitchen needs even more help downsizing than our closet! So, let's get started.

Why do we waste so much food?
Which of the excuses below resonate with you?

- I'm busy, so I eat out a lot, and food I've purchased expires.

- I forget what's in my pantry and fridge, often until after it's expired.

- My fridge and pantry are so full that I can't really see everything I have.

- Restaurant portions are often too large for me, so I usually throw part of them away.

- Items look appetizing in the grocery store, but I just don't get around to eating them once I bring them home.

- I try to buy healthier food, but then I don't eat it.

- I rarely get around to eating leftovers.

- I'm too tired around mealtime, so unless it's a meal I can make quickly, I often don't get around to making it—even though I've purchased all of the ingredients.

- When items are on sale, I stock up. But they often expire before I can use them.

- I like the idea of cooking, more than actually doing it.

Other reasons:

_____

_____

_____

_____

_____

_____

_____

_____

We don't change our habits unless we're convinced there's a real benefit to making that change. Spend a few moments thinking about the main reason you waste food. Then, write down what action steps you will take to downsize your grocery budget—by downsizing how much you waste.

_____

_____

_____

_____

_____

_____

_____

_____

_____

_____

_____

Here are a few ideas you may want to consider trying, as well:

- Eat leftovers the day after you make them. They'll be less likely to disappear toward the back of the fridge. They'll also be fresher and more appetizing.

- Invite friends over for dinner when you make a big meal, so there won't be any leftovers!

- Order your groceries online, where there's less chance for you to impulse buy.

- Keep no more than one "back-up" on hand of any item.

- If you shop at a membership warehouse where items are often oversized, go with a friend and divide your purchase.

- Hold a Pantry Party, where friends and family bring items from their pantry that they haven't used (that haven't reached their expiration date) and trade!

- Don't use a large cart when you shop. Use a small cart or carry a personal shopping bag or basket. (Using your own bag or basket will also save you from using paper or plastic bags to carry your groceries home. Double win!) To do this, you'll need to shop more often than once a week. Shopping more frequently allows you to buy smaller amounts of produce, which will have less chance of spoiling before you have a chance to eat it.

- Write a grocery list and stick to it!

A PEEK INTO YOUR PANTRY

Many people searching for a new home hope to find one that includes a walk-in pantry. A pantry can be a definite asset, even in a downsized home. Ideally, you open a door, see what you have on hand, and grab what you need. But not everyone's pantry meets that ideal. Some are more like black holes, filled with items you don't use and don't even remember you have.

The less organized your pantry is, the less useful it is. Also, the more food you probably waste. So, let's make a clean sweep. You know the drill. Take every item out of your pantry and set it on your table or counter. If your pantry demands a bit more "breathing room," put a clean sheet on the floor and place all of your items there. Then start sorting.

How you organize your pantry is a bit like how you organized your cupboards and drawers. Put items together in groups that make sense to you. Perhaps you'll have a breakfast section, a snack section, a baking section, etc. Or maybe you prefer to put boxes all in one area and cans in another.

Then, section-by-section, check the expiration dates. From here on out, you'll be wasting less food by using up items before they expire! Sort each group into smaller groups: Keep, Discard and Donate.

Remember, keep only one back-up item for every opened item—unless it's something you eat multiples of each week. Put all of the other multiples aside to donate to a local soup kitchen or homeless shelter.

Before you put the items you wish to keep back in the pantry, wipe down each shelf with a non-toxic cleaner. (Since you'll be placing food back on these shelves, it's best not to use your heavy-duty bathroom cleanser! Half-water mixed with half-vinegar works great.) Then, sweep, vacuum, or scrub the pantry floor. Whatever you prefer. If you're a shelf-liner aficionado, now's the time to line your clean, dry shelves with the liner of your choice.

Then, starting at eye level, place the group of items you use most frequently. Put the oldest containers toward the front. (Every time you go grocery shopping, put the new item behind older ones, so you'll use those with the oldest expiration dates first.) If your pantry shelves are deep (over 16"), consider storing items on rolling pantry trays. That way you can have access to see what's hiding in the back of your pantry, so it's less likely to be forgotten or wasted. If your shelves have an overabundance of space between them, use stacking shelves, or clip-on baskets that hang below the shelves, to maximize your space.

Place boxes (such as cereal) sideways—spine out—like a book, to save space. Group smaller items, such as packets of ketchup or soy sauce saved from take-out meals, in small, plastic containers. (Remember, just because it's "free" doesn't mean you have to take it with you and stash it away for future generations. Take only what you need. Use whatever you take!)

Reserve the top shelf, which is often inaccessible without a stepstool, for any nonfood items you may want to store in your pantry, such as laundry and cleaning products. This will keep them out of the reach of children and pets. That shelf is also a handy spot to store seldom-used serving pieces, such as a punch bowl or ice bucket.

Don't forget that the inside of your pantry door also holds potential storage space. Hang an organizer for rolls of foil, baking parchment, and plastic wrap. Or use that space to hang your broom and dustpan, family calendar, or spice rack.

> **HINT: Spices are expensive, so treat them with respect!**
> **They need to be kept tightly closed in a cool, dark, dry spot,**
> **away from direct heat and sunlight. In other words, your pantry is**
> **the perfect place to store them. Although spices may not change in**
> **appearance over time, they do lose their flavor—which is why you use**
> **them in the first place. You can keep whole spices about 4 years, ground**
> **spices for 2 to 3 years, and dried herbs for 1 to 3 years. If you want to**
> **keep track of how old your spices are, put a colored sticker on the bottle**
> **when you buy it. Have a different color for each year. Of course, one sure**
> **fire way to know if your spices have reached their expiration date is that**
> **if spices have lost their aroma, they've lost their flavor! Toss them.**

THE WELL-STOCKED FRIDGE

Your refrigerator is just like your pantry, only chillier! However, when it's overfilled, it can't work up to its full potential. Food needs cold air to circulate around it to keep it cool. If you've crammed so much inside that trying to put your hands on one particular item means taking lots of other items out first, and then putting them all back after your search and rescue mission is complete, both you and your fridge are wasting energy.

If clutter-control is in order, follow the same basic system you used to downsize your pantry, only put a little spring in your step as you work. You'll want to get these items back into their temperature-controlled environment as soon as possible. Also, wait until you've finished sorting your refrigerated goods before tackling your frozen foods.

If you have young children at home, or grandkids who visit frequently, why not invite them to help you clean out the fridge? They don't need to know it's considered a chore. It makes a perfect game! Not only is it more fun to do together, it also helps kids master a few clutter-free habits they can use in the future. It may even help them be a bit more thoughtful when they're putting items away in the fridge from now on. Refer to your fridge purge as a treasure hunt or matching game. Once you've taken all of the items out, ask the kids to search for expired items to toss, put multiples of the same item together, and then group items that go together, like different kinds of cheese, yogurts, or vegetables. While they're doing this, you can give the fridge a good scrub with a non-toxic cleanser, so it's ready for you to put the items you want to keep back in a more organized manner. When it's time to put everything back, have them hand you the items you need as you need them. If you're feeling creative, you can give them clues, such as, "Hand me everything that grows on a tree" or "Hand me all of the cheese, from the lightest color to the darkest color." Whether it's cleaning the fridge, sorting laundry, or organizing a bookshelf, never underestimate how a little creativity can turn a chore into a time of bonding, and learning, for the kids in your life.

Once you've emptied your fridge, wiped down the inside, and you're ready to put the things you want to keep back inside, it's time to ask yourself an important question: Do I know how to use my fridge? That may seem like a ridiculous question. You put stuff in it and then shut the door. Done. But today's modern-day refrigerator is much more than an old-time icebox. The temperature we have our refrigerator set at and where we place the items inside will determine how well our refrigerator can do its job.

First, temperature. The ideal temperature for a refrigerator is 35 to 40 degrees. Anything below 35 and items near the back may start to freeze. Anything above 40 degrees and the bacteria growth on the food inside will triple. How full you keep your refrigerator will also help determine how cold you should keep it. The fuller the fridge, the colder you'll need to set the temp. If your refrigerator has a temperature dial that ranges from 1 to 5, 5 will be the coldest. If you keep your fridge relatively full on a regular basis, set the dial between 3 and 4. If you only keep the bare necessities inside (or are headed out on vacation), set the dial between 2 and 3.

As for what to put where, your fridge is like your home. Heat rises, so the warmest place will be near the top and the coldest near the bottom. Also, anything you put in the shelves in the door will be in the warmest spot of your fridge.

Here's a little cheat-sheet on the best place to store common items in your fridge:

EGGS: Store them where the temperature is most consistent—on the middle shelf.

MILK: This needs to be where it's coldest, which means never store it in the door. Put it on the bottom shelf, in the back. It will stay fresh longer.

YOGURT, SOUR CREAM, COTTAGE CHEESE: Like milk, these last longest when kept in the coldest spot, bottom shelf near the back.

BUTTER, SOFT CHEESE: These are well-suited for the butter/dairy compartment on the door of your fridge.

CONDIMENTS: Items like salad dressings, ketchup, and mayonnaise contain natural preservatives like salt and vinegar. That means they can join pickles and salsa on the shelves of your refrigerator door.

NUT OILS: Unlike olive and vegetable oil, these cannot be kept in your pantry. They can go on a shelf on your refrigerator door.

ORANGE JUICE: This can go on the door IF it's pasteurized. If it's fresh-squeezed, store it on the bottom shelf where it's colder.

DELI MEATS: They are what the shallow meat drawer was designed for! It's slightly colder than the rest of the fridge. If you don't have a deli drawer, put them on the bottom shelf.

PACKAGED RAW MEAT: If you are not freezing your meat, or if you are thawing meat from the freezer, keep it on the coldest, lower shelf. That will also help prevent any drips from contaminating what's below it in the fridge.

VEGETABLES: There are usually two drawers at the bottom of the fridge. One is for fruit and the other for vegetables. If you can adjust the humidity, keep the vegetables in the one with higher humidity to keep them moist. Remember, potatoes, tomatoes and onions never go in the fridge. Keep them in your pantry, a fruit/vegetable basket on the counter, or in a kitchen drawer designated for veggies.

FRUITS: These go in the other drawer, with lower humidity. Remember, if it wilts it requires higher humidity and if it rots it needs lower humidity! Also, do not wash fruits and vegetables before putting them in the fridge. Water can encourage mold and bacteria growth.

A couple of other quick tips for a fabulous fridge:

- Before you head to the grocery store, move everything from the back of the fridge to the front. That way you don't purchase something you already have.

- When you bring home groceries, put the newly purchased items behind any like items already in your fridge. That way you finish up the oldest items first.

- Keep leftovers for four days tops. It's best to keep them in glass containers, so you can easily see what you have.

- Keep an open container of baking soda at the back of the fridge to keep it smelling fresh.

- For all of you shelf-liner fans, here's another chance to use your favorite product. Just make certain it's water-proof and easy-to-clean. Removable liners, see-through plastic bins, can dispensers, turntables, and even clear plastic shoe containers, can help keep your fridge clean and organized.

HINT: Remember the Swedish fulskåp, alias "cabinet for the ugly"? Sometimes, the unwanted gifts we receive are edible. Or, at least, the person who gave them to us intended them to be. But just because we receive food doesn't mean we're obligated to eat it. Fruit cake may be our kryptonite. Our borderline diabetes may preclude us from snarfing an entire pound of Aunt Martha's fudge. (Or it should!) We may not care for jalapeno pepper jam. We may not want to go to the trouble of making bread with the gift of sourdough starter. Whatever our reason, instead of simply waiting until our edible gift goes bad and then throwing it out, let's do our best to use it. Bring it to a potluck, have friends over and add it to the buffet.

DON'T FORGET THE FREEZER

Believe it or not, frozen food will retain most of its nutrition almost indefinitely. As for its flavor and texture, well, that's another story. After about three months, most items will begin to show signs of freezer burn. That doesn't mean you shouldn't eat it. If it was safe to eat before it was frozen, and it's been kept frozen, it's safe to eat once it's thawed. But just because you can eat something doesn't mean you want to.

That's why it's good to get in the habit of being as pro-active about using the food in your freezer as the food in your pantry and fridge. Just because it doesn't sport an expiration date, doesn't mean you should pass down an antique frozen pot roast to your kids. Stick with passing down the recipe.

One thing that can help organize your freezer is using clear plastic bins in your freezer, as well as your refrigerator. Put all of the frozen veggies in one, meats in another, frozen meals in another, etc. That way you can pull an entire bin out of the freezer to see what you have, instead of starting an arctic avalanche by trying to extricate a pound of rock-hard ground beef that's buried in the back of your freezer.

Like your fridge, your freezer has a few "best use" practices. Do you know them? First, like your fridge, it runs most efficiently when full. But that doesn't mean that you have to make an exception to your new Think Small attitude and stock up on a side of beef. If your freezer is particularly barren, add water bottles. Not only will it help your freezer run well, you'll have bottles ready to use in a cooler or to take for a hike on a hot day.

There are a few foods that are not recommended to freeze. Many of these foods, particularly those with a high-water content (like fresh fruits and veggies) turn to mush if frozen.

FOODS YOU SHOULD NEVER FREEZE:

- Raw fruits and vegetables (Although there are a few exceptions listed under Freezer Hacks)

- Yogurt, and sour cream (Freezing will change taste and texture.)

- Mayonnaise and mayo-based salads, such as chicken, tuna, ham, egg, and macaroni

- Eggs in the shell

- Egg-white based frostings, or meringue pies

- Hard boiled eggs

- Fried foods (They'll turn into a soggy mess!)

- Ground spices (They'll become more concentrated and taste bitter when used.)

- Gelatin

A Couple of Quick Freezer Hacks:

- If you're going to freeze cooked pasta, undercook it, so it won't turn quite so mushy when it's frozen.

- Although you shouldn't freeze fresh eggs in their shells, you can take the egg out of the shell, put it in a freezer bag, and keep it in the freezer for up to a year. Thaw it in your fridge before using.

- You can freeze fresh berries if you put them on a cookie sheet in a single layer. Once they're frozen, transfer them to a freezer bag. You can do the same with tomatoes. Just place parchment paper on the cookie sheet first.

- If your ice cream is too hard to scoop, heat a sharp knife under warm water. Then, make a grid with the warmed knife with one-inch squares, one inch deep. Poof! Scoop-able!

HINT: Unless you're an avid hunter, or you regularly buy a side of beef to feed your family of 10, having a freezer in the garage in addition to the one that comes with your fridge, is not conducive to Thinking Small. It's hoarding food, plain and simple. Also, a freezer needs to be kept filled to run efficiently. Chances are pretty good that whatever is at the back or at the bottom is not going to be consumed in the next three months.

If you're wondering how long you can keep items in the freezer before they start losing their texture and flavor. Here is a FREEZING CHART for quick reference.

ITEM	MONTHS
Fruits	
Home frozen	10
Canned fruits, opened	2
Juices	12
Citrus fruits	4-6
Vegetables	
Home frozen	10
Purchased frozen	8

ITEM	MONTHS
Breads & Baked Goods	
Cookies, muffins, breads	6-12
Unfrosted cakes	3
Fruit Pies	6-8
Pumpkin or chiffon pies	1-2
Unbaked rolls & breads	1
Cookie dough	3

ITEM	MONTHS	ITEM	MONTHS

Dairy & Eggs

Butter, margarine	9
Milk	1-3
Cheese, (cottage, ricotta, cream)	1
Cheese, (natural or processed)	6-8
Cream, light	1
Cream, heavy	NR
Ice Cream, ice milk	2-4
Eggs, in shell	NR

Meat, Fresh Roast, Steaks, Chops

Beef	6-12
Veal, pork	4-9
Lamb	6-9
Ground meats, stew meat	3-4
Sausage	1-2
Cooked meat dishes	2-3
Gravy & broth	2-3
Canned, open	NR
Soups, stews	4-6

Meat, Proccessed & Cured

Bacon	1
Frankfurters	1-2
Ham (whole, half)	1-2
Ham (canned, unopened)	NR
Luncheon Meats	1-2

Poultry, Fresh

Chicken, turkey (whole)	12
Chicken, turkey (pieces)	6-8
Duck, goose (whole)	6

Poultry, Cooked

Cooked poultry dishes	1-6
Pieces in broth	6
Pieces not in broth	1
Fried chicken	4

Seafood

Clams, oysters (shucked), scallops	3-4
Crab	2
Shrimp, lobster	6-12
Freshwater fish	6-9
Fillets	4-6
Salmon steaks	2
Cooked fish	1

A WORD ABOUT COUPONING

With all of this focus on food, grocery shopping easily comes to mind. If you want to downsize your budget, spending less at the grocery store is a worthy goal. One way you can accomplish that goal is by using coupons. Most grocery stores offer a loyalty program, where you can save money by simply downloading coupons and using a card or app at the store. Many shoppers stop right there. You might be one of them.

However, with a little time and effort you can save additional money by couponing. Whether you choose to use a digital coupon website or app, or to scan the Sunday paper—scissors in hand—clipping coupons the "old-fashioned" way, is up to you. It really boils down to which is most comfortable, convenient, and enjoyable for you—as well, as which coupons you will actually use.

Obviously, using digital coupons will prevent additional paper chaos in your home. They also may prove more convenient, because they're downloaded onto your phone, so they're always close at hand. They also disappear once they expire, saving you the painstaking process of tossing coupons that are no longer valid.

However, if you continue to find coupon clipping a relaxing, money-saving habit, don't let digital peer pressure force you to change your ways. Just don't waste your time (and your time IS money) by clipping them and then forgetting them. Put them in a file folder or coupon wallet, organized by category. For instance, have a section for groceries (food items), groceries (non-food items), fast food, restaurants, local attractions, services, etc. In true downsizing fashion, only clip what you will actually use. Stick to products you already use on a regular basis, ones you'll redeem before they expire.

It's dealing with the unused, expired coupons that's the most time-consuming and clutter-causing part of the couponing process. Every time you add coupons, toss any that have expired. And remember, you control your coupons. They do not control you. If you have a stack of coupons you haven't had time to sort through, don't feel obligated to look through them all. Toss them into recycling and start clipping again next week.

HINT: Go paperless by signing up for automatic bill pay whenever possible. Not only will you save a tree, you'll save yourself the hassle of forgetting to pay a bill while on vacation or paying a late fee because of absentmindedness.

A few money-saving reminders:

- There are lots of popular coupon apps. Try them out to see which works best for you. Delete the rest.

- Check out cashback websites for rebates on purchases.

- Buy discounted gift cards and use them for your purchases (grocery, retail, and restaurants).

- If you really want to get serious about savings, check out blogs by writers who research which items are on sale every week at which stores.

- Base your weekly menu from what's on sale at your local grocery store.

- Make the most of your time by clipping coupons while watching any TV shows that don't demand your full attention.

- Always shop with a list. Star each item you have a coupon for, to help remind yourself to redeem the coupon when you check out.

- Some big box stores offer a debit card that entitles you to a discount every time you shop. Signing up for one is free and helps prevent you from carrying a balance on your credit card. It also saves you money without any extra thought or effort.

- Unless you pay off your balance every month, quit using credit cards altogether. Use an envelope system where you divide cash into envelopes for your monthly purchases. When the envelope is empty, you have to wait until the following month to make that purchase.

- Implement a 30-day rule on major, or impulse-driven, purchases. If after 30 days you still feel good about buying it, go for it. You'll find that by waiting, you'll purchase less.

- Remember that your time is not free. When couponing begins to feel more like a job than a hobby, reevaluate your couponing habits. Is the money you save worth the time and gas you spend?

OPEN TO THE PUBLIC

Once you've tackled the rooms and storage areas in your home that seem to accumulate the most clutter, it's time to move on to the more public rooms, like the living room, family room, or den. Even the entryway is worthy of a second look. Is every piece of furniture necessary? Do any of them look worn, faded, or dirty? Does every knickknack give you joy? Does the room feel too cluttered or busy to be restful? If you have a living room and a family room, do you really need a television in both?

Survey these "living areas" with a critical eye. Just because something has been in the same spot forever doesn't mean it has to stay that way. Maybe it's time to shake things up a bit, give your living room a new look without breaking the budget.

Here are a few easy and affordable ways to add new life to your living areas:

- Update family photos. Baby photos are fine, but if Jr. now has kids of his own, perhaps it's time to switch out a few of the older photographs or pair an older photo with a recent one.

- Add new throw pillows to an older couch.

- If your flooring looks worn, add a new throw rug. Put a dark rug on light flooring or carpet and a light rug on dark flooring or carpet.

- Paint one wall an accent color and add coordinating cushions throughout the room.

- Add a pop of color to the edge of a door or window frame.

- Fill an unused fireplace with an arrangement of candles or faux flowers.

- Cover up on old sofa with a colorful throw.

- Paint a coffee table.

- Cut down on clutter by putting magazines, newspapers, or remotes in decorative baskets. Be sure to recycle anything that is not in use!

- Swap out light switch covers with something fun and decorative.

- Switch lamps from one room to another.

- Change out lampshades.

- Hang plates on the wall.

- Put up shelves to display favorite (downsized!) collectibles.

- Add a few houseplants (Stick to fake ones, if you'd rather dust than water.)

- Reorganize your bookshelves.

- Instead of having all of your books lined up vertically, break up the line with a horizontal stack here and there.

- Paint the back of your bookcase with an accent color.

- Arrange books by the color of their spine.

- Don't fill a shelf all the way to the end. Add decorative bookends and then put a bowl of found items, such as shells or stones, on the shelf, as well.

- Add artwork or photos in between groupings of books.

ALL BOOKED UP

Speaking of books, they're another possession that seems to multiply as we age. It's easy to just keep adding to our collection. We finish reading a book. We put it on the shelf. We don't touch it again until we move. Then, we bemoan the fact that our boxes of books weigh almost as much as our sleeper sofa.

If you're a reader, periodically downsizing your bookcase is as important as regularly sorting through your bedroom closet. Just because you love a book doesn't mean you have an obligation to own a copy.

Tackle your bookcases the same way you did your bedroom closet. Ask yourself:

- Will I read this again?

- If I lost this book, would I notice it's missing?

- Would I spend the time and effort necessary to replace it?

- Do I actually enjoy owning this book or am I holding onto it because I enjoyed reading it?

- Is this book like a prom dress, something that holds more memories than it does actual value to me right now?

- Do I have any duplicate copies? If I have a hardcover and a paper back, am I going to use both—or either—of these in the future?

- Do I refer to this book regularly for work or other personal reasons? If so, would it be advantageous to purchase a copy online that won't wear out and doesn't take up space on my bookshelf?

- Like the other "antiques" I've reevaluated in my home, does this hold real value (monetary or emotional) or is it simply old?

Now that you have a stack of books you no longer use, what can you do with them? Here are a few ideas:

- Donate them to libraries. They often sell used books as fundraisers.

- Sell them to used bookstores for a little extra cash.

- Take them to a "Little Free Library" in your area, where people can choose any books they'd like for free.

- Donate books to your local charity thrift shop.

- Find out whether any schools, community centers, shelters, or prisons accept used books in your area.

- Check out nonprofit organizations that donate books to readers around the world.

- Invite friends over for a book party, where they can shop your shelves for free.

THE DIGITAL DILEMMA

One answer to overflowing bookshelves is to purchase e-books, instead of physical books from here on out. Instead of taking up shelf space, they simply take up cyber space. However, just because you can't see clutter, doesn't mean it isn't there. If you aren't careful, you can end up with a cluttered cyber mess, where it's as hard to find what you're looking for as it was when your home was overflowing with excess.

Whether it's your e-reader, phone, computer, or downloaded movies and recorded programs on your television, take time to delete what you don't need or use. When your computers, phones, and DVRs remind you that you're running out of space, it's time to purge. Paying to buy more memory is simply your digital age's version of procrastination.

Check This Out

Weigh the pros and cons between owning physical books, DVDs, and CDs, as opposed to digital books, movies, and music. Obviously, storing—and moving—digital collections are a lot less of a hassle. But if you don't use them, you're perpetuating your tendency to acquire and hoard as much as if you could hold these virtual objects in your hands. Downsizing is as much of a mental discipline as it is a physical one. Being content with less is what truly allows you to live a bigger, richer, fuller life. To do this takes more than simply sorting, discarding, and redistributing. It takes some honest soul-searching. Is there a hole in your heart you're trying to fill with "stuff"? Once you address what you're truly lacking, you find the source of your discontent. It isn't how much you own or what you own. It's your relationship to it. Strive to break the habit of "loving" stuff. It will never love you back.

MAKING THE MOVE

If downsizing includes a move to a new home (whether it's totally new or simply new to you!), CONGRATULATIONS! Talk about a fresh slate! But even after downsizing what you own, moving what's left can still prove a herculean task. Whether you're moving across the country, or across town, you still have to pack it all, and figure out how to transport all of the odds and ends that you've deemed important enough to make the journey with you. After doing so, you may be tempted to downsize even more!

To help make your move go as smoothly as possible, here are a few quick and easy moving hacks:

- **Print off one of the many moving schedules available online. It will remind you when to take care of things like starting and stopping your utilities, forwarding your mail, etc.**

- **Before purchasing boxes, try your best to secure some for free. Contact office supply stores, bookstores, pharmacies, etc., and ask for any boxes they are going to recycle. Also, many recycling centers have a section where people drop off carboard boxes for reuse. There are also online forums and message exchanges where people offer free boxes. If you need to purchase boxes, do so from a company that allows you to return boxes you don't use.**

- **After using your boxes, try to pass them on to another person on the move, or recycle them.**

- **Instead of purchasing more expensive boxes with built-in handles, cut a triangle in each box about 1/3 of the way down from the top, big enough for your hand to fit. Voila! A free instant handle.**

- **Put all of your packing materials (packing tape, scissors, marker or color-coded stickers, packing paper or plastic, etc.) in a basket you can easily carry from room-to-room as you pack.**

- Remove furniture dents from the carpet by letting an ice cube melt in the dent. Then fluff the fibers with a spoon.

- Pack nonessentials first. Or, start by packing the room you use least.

- Fill empty space in boxes with plastic grocery bags. The less room there is for items to move in the box, the less likelihood there is of them breaking.

- Put plastic wrap around drawers, so you don't have to empty them to move a dresser.

- Put jewelry in empty egg cartons to prevent tangling. Even if you try to keep a jewelry case vertical, if you have to go up or down any stairs, everything inside can end up a tangled mess.

- Keep clothing on hangers and put sections of them inside trash bags. Poke the hangers through the bottom of the bag. Close the open end with a twist tie. This is a more practical alternative to bulky, expensive wardrobe boxes.

- Newspaper can bleed and ruin items, as well as leave your hands an inky mess. Use white newsprint paper (which is like craft or drawing paper).

- Or get creative with packing material. Use clean socks to protect glasses and stemware. Use towels, clothing, jackets, bedding, tablecloths, and cushions as packing material.

- Place paper towels between plates to cushion them, then line them up vertically to prevent breakage.

- Put plastic wrap under the caps of any liquids to prevent leaks.

- Remove printer ink and toner before moving, so they don't break or spill during transport.

- Use all of your suitcases and bags, instead of extra boxes. Transport heavy items, such as books, in suitcases with wheels.

- Use toilet paper tubes to hold cords and cables. Be sure to label what they are used for.

- Cover razors with binder clips to keep from getting cut when removing them.

- Keep hardware for shelves, etc. in labeled, ziplocked plastic bags.

- Use color-coded stickers to designate which room each box goes to. Number the boxes and keep a general list of what's inside, so if you need to locate something quickly once you've moved, you can.

- Fill pots and pans with bottles of spices to keep them from breaking.

- If you're moving knives that do not have a sheath, put them inside a potholder and secure the bottom with a rubber band.

- Instead of purchasing mattress and box springs moving bags, simply put a fitted sheet over each side.

- Use pool noodles to protect the frames of artwork or large mirrors. Cut the noodle down its length and slip over the edge of the frame. Put a masking tape X across the center of any glass you are transporting to keep it from breaking.

- Before moving your entertainment center, take a picture of how the wires and cables are connected. Label each cable before disconnecting.

- Pack large, heavy items at the bottom and toward the front of the truck.

- Keep a basket, or OPEN ME FIRST box, that contains essential items such as toiletries, toilet paper, a couple changes of clothing, bedding, a box cutter for opening boxes, a coffee maker and coffee... whatever will help make you feel right at home, and ready to get to work on settling in, once you arrive.

THE HOSPITABLE HOME

The word "hospitality," which carries both Latin and French roots, is tied to the word "hospital." Back in the day (about 1560), a hospital was a guest chamber or lodging. It's where guests—whether friends or strangers— were cared for. Whether you're moving to a new address, or getting your current abode under clutter-control, having a home that feels warm and inviting is important—if not for guests, at least for you!

Some people seem to have been born with the hospitality gene. For them, having others over for a meal or to spend the night is an occasion they anticipate with great energy and joy. Others prefer to be a guest, rather than a host. Yes, they may have friends and family over from time to time. However, opening their home feels more like work than joy, more draining than energizing. Still others, prefer their home be a solitary island retreat. For them, socializing is reserved for birthdays and Christmas parties, preferably celebrated anywhere other than where they live.

There's no right or wrong as to how hospitable you are. It's more a matter of personal preference and comfort. However, your hospitality level does play a part in your downsizing plans. If having people over makes your heart sing, you need to maintain some room to entertain. That doesn't mean you have to have a separate guest room, or a dining room as opposed to an eat-in kitchen. With a little bit of space, and a lot of creativity, downsizing and hospitality can be perfectly compatible.

If you're moving to a smaller home, consider combining an office and guest room into one. Install a Murphy bed or wall bed to save space. Or, purchase an inflatable bed, preferably one on a frame that can be easily rolled into the corner of a closet or garage for storage. When overnight guests are on your agenda, simply move furniture in the living room or dining area to accommodate the bed. Although it may not afford much privacy, hospitality isn't about the size of the room or luxury of the accommodations. It's about making others feel welcome and at home.

Save travel-sized toiletries, and free toothbrushes from your dental visits, to make available to guests, if they need them. Keep regional maps and coupons for local attractions in a "guest" basket. Keep a small chalkboard to set by your guest's bed and leave a personalized welcome message. And don't forget to put a chocolate, homemade treat, or little welcome gift on your guest's pillow to let them know how glad you are to share your home with them.

Check This Out   Placing a memory foam pad under the sheets of an inflatable bed will prevent it from feeling overly cold at night.

TIPS FOR SMALL SPACE ENTERTAINING

- Before you make your guest list, consider how many people you can realistically, and comfortably, fit into the space you have available to entertain.

- Remember, serving a sit-down dinner requires more space than having people mingle over appetizers. Let the number of people you're inviting help dictate your menu.

- Move your kitchen or dining room table to a back room—or push it up against the wall to use as a buffet. Place folding chairs in the newly available space.

- Remove everything from your countertops (including a mixer, fruit bowl, and coffee maker—unless it will be used for the party). Use the extra space as a drink/food buffet.

- Remove books from bookshelves and use the shelves as buffet space.

- Use cake stands (borrow a few, if necessary) to provide more serving space at different levels.

- Designate a specific spot for coats and purses beforehand. An easy-to-store portable clothing rack may be a good solution.

- Small spaces heat up quickly when occupied by lots of people! Remember to open a window, set up a fan, or provide access to a patio for guests, if things get too toasty.

- Set up food and drinks in two separate areas to keep guests from bunching up in one spot.

- Have all food prepared beforehand, so you can enjoy your guests and not spend your time cooking.

- If your guests would be comfortable sitting on the floor, borrow cushions and have a picnic on the carpet.

- Consider providing a few dishes that are gluten-free, dairy-free, and vegetarian, for guests with diet constraints.

- Keep the event low-stress on your end. Don't try a new recipe for the first time or prepare a dish that leaves your entire kitchen in shambles. Hospitality isn't about impressing others. It's about creating a space where others can feel at home and enjoy themselves—whether that space is big or small.

- Don't forget to enjoy yourself!

OUR FOUR-LEGGED FRIENDS

There are some relationships that demand very little of us. These often include our pets. But caring for a pet is not responsibility-free. It takes time to feed them, groom them, walk them, clean up after them, or do whatever else is required to keep them happy and healthy. When we go on vacation, or sometimes even when we wind up having to stay late at work, we're also forced to call on others to help meet our pets' basic needs. It takes a portion of our budget to pay for vet bills, to supply our furry or feathered friends with food, and to purchase those cute little costumes we make them wear during the holidays. As a matter of fact, the estimated annual cost to care for a dog is about $1200, and $1000 a year to care for a cat. That amount is far from chicken feed.

When we decide to downsize, especially if that decision requires a move, it may require us to consider our pets' part in that plan. If we're renting, some apartments, condos, and townhomes do not allow pets. Others charge an extra fee to allow them to live there. If we're buying, the square footage of our new home—or the fact that there is no yard—may make pet ownership more of a challenge.

If you are not currently a pet owner but have been thinking about adopting a pet, keep these considerations in mind. The decision is a personal one. However, if the responsibility of being a pet owner is concerning, it doesn't mean your pet days are over.

Consider these alternatives:

- Volunteer at a rescue shelter.

- Research local options for renting a pet for a day. (Yes, they do exist!)

- Visit a Cat Café, where hanging out with furry friends is actually on the menu!

- Become a dog walker or pet sit for friends and neighbors. Not only will this add a bit of extra cash to your budget but help fill your quotient of critter cuddles in the process.

OLD DOGS AND NEW TRICKS

In 1523, a book on animal husbandry stated that dogs should be taught herding behaviors when they're pups, because it's more difficult for them to master them when they're older. From this humble beginning, one of the oldest proverbial sayings in the English language was born: "You can't teach an old dog new tricks." However, just because something may be more difficult, doesn't mean it can't be done!

If we've grown up—and grown older and more comfortable—in habits that foster clutter, it can take some time and effort to adapt to a more minimalist, clutter-free lifestyle. And even after we've worked hard to diligently downsize our possessions and the size of our home, once we've settled in, it's fairly easy to slide back into our former rut of accumulating and procrastinating. Before we know it, we're back to square one, forced to start once more at the beginning of this book, faced with a closet that's overflowing with clothing we don't wear, items we don't use, and purchases we wish we hadn't made.

Thinking Small isn't a short-term project. It's a lifelong process. Like losing weight, quitting an unhealthy habit, or adopting a more active lifestyle, it's a goal that takes ongoing maintenance.

Here are a few quick and easy habits we can practice each day to help us maintain the freedom that downsizing our lives has afforded us:

- **Make your bed every morning. As you do, recommit to doing your best to keep clutter under control throughout the day.**

- **Don't use your fridge as an art gallery or magnetic calendar. Once things begin to look cluttered, it's easier for yet more clutter to blend right in!**

- **Don't put things down. Put them away.**

- **Only handle mail once. Toss it, recycle it, file it, or act on it.**

- Take a few minutes after each meal to wash the dishes or put them in the dishwasher, before food sticks to them. Keeping the sink and kitchen counters clean and clear will reduce stress and effort when it's time to prepare your next meal.

- Have a designated place for everything!

- Do fast jobs (anything under two minutes) immediately. Take out the trash. Wipe up the crumbs on the counter. Put the remote back where it belongs. Put your clothes in the hamper. Hang the towel on the rack.

- Do one chore a day, such as mop the floor or clean toilets. Or, set aside one hour on the weekends where you turn on music and clean everything you can in that time period.

- Keep a small donation box by your back door or in the garage. As you go through your month and see things in your home that you don't need, want, or use, add them to your box. Make a monthly charity drop-off run with its contents.

- If you have children or grandchildren in your home, help them gain clutter-free habits by making clean-up time a game, instead of a chore. Before mealtimes, naptimes, and/ or bedtime, turn on a "clean up" song, during which they have to hustle to put everything away in its proper place.

- Only shop for what you need, not for entertainment.

- Put your home "to bed" at night. (Think of it as the bookend to making your bed in the morning.) Take a few minutes to put everything in its proper place before you retire. You'll sleep better, knowing you'll wake up to a home that's well-cared for and in order.

- Keep possessions from accumulating by following a "one in, one out" policy. If you buy a new pair of shoes, one has got to go. This will prevent you from having to continually purge your closet.

- Keep your discretionary spending under control. Take your monthly income, subtract your fixed expenses (include money you add to savings or investments and regularly donate to charity) and then divide what's left by 30. That's the amount you have available to spend every day. If you don't spend it, that amount rolls over to the next day. Challenge yourself to see if you can have more left at the end of each month than you did the month before! Save that money for a rainy day or for a larger "luxury" item. Give it to someone in need. Use it for vacations. Whatever you decide is best!

- Unsubscribe from online retail websites. Seeing email deals pop up every morning can entice you to purchase things you don't need, just because they're on sale.

- Make a list before you shop and only purchase what's on the list. Or, follow the "think about it for 30 days" plan. If you still want after a month has passed, then buy it.

- Change your perspective on cleaning and clutter control. Instead of viewing it as a chore, view it as a gift you give yourself, a key to less stress and responsibility, one that opens a door to a freer, more fulfilling life.

- Challenge yourself to "no spend" seasons. You set the rules. For instance, don't buy coffee on the way to work for a month or don't buy any new clothing for six months. Try not to spend any money for a week—only use what you have. Don't shop for groceries for a week—try to use up everything in your pantry and freezer. These little exercises in restraint can help consumerism loosen its hold on your lifestyle.

LOOKING BACK

It's time to celebrate how far you've come! Look back over your Vision Statement at the beginning of the book. Then, take a few moments to consider the questions below.

How well have you fulfilled your Vision Statement?

_____

_____

_____

_____

_____

_____

_____

_____

_____

_____

_____

_____

_____

_____

_____

_____

_____

_____

_____

_____

_____

_____

_____

What would you still like to accomplish?

_____

_____

_____

_____

_____

_____

_____

_____

_____

_____

How has Thinking Small expanded your life?

_____

_____

_____

_____

_____

_____

_____

_____

_____

_____

Looking for simple ways to shrink your ecological footprint?

Here are a few ideas to get you started:

- Don't buy bottled water. Use your own refillable water bottle.

- Bring your own reusable bags to the grocery store.

- Lower your thermostat by one degree in the winter and raise it by one degree in the summer. You may not even be able to tell the difference, but it could save you between 1 and 3% on your heating bill, while saving energy at the same time.

- Place a plastic bottle filled with water in your toilet tank. You'll save water with every flush!

- Avoid "vampire power." Unplug what you're not using.

- Don't purchase paper towels. Use washable rags, instead.

- Go to the library or purchase e-books, instead of buying books—which use over 30 million trees a year.

- Wash clothes in cold water.

- Go paperless on all of your bills, your newspaper, and your magazine subscriptions.

- Eat more sustainable seafood, which has a smaller carbon footprint than other sources of protein.

- Choose energy efficient appliances.

- Choose second-hand or recycled furnishings.

- Use biodegradable, non-toxic cleaning products.

- Shop your local farmer's market. Eat locally and in season!

- Drive less. Walk, bike, or take public transportation.

- If you need a car, Think Small and keep it well-maintained to reduce emissions.

- Buy less!

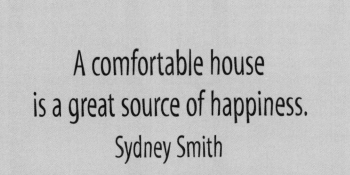

A comfortable house
is a great source of happiness.
Sydney Smith